STONEWALL JACKSON
LEE'S GREATEST LIEUTENANT

THE HISTORY OF THE CIVIL WAR

THE HISTORY OF THE CIVIL WAR

STONEWALL JACKSON

LEE'S GREATEST LIEUTENANT

by BARBARA J. BENNETT

INTRODUCTORY ESSAY BY
HENRY STEELE COMMAGER

SILVER BURDETT PRESS

To Thomas P. Whitney

Series Editorial Supervisor: Richard G. Gallin
Series Editing: Agincourt Press
Series Consultant: Elizabeth Fortson
Cover and Text Design: Circa 86, New York
Series Supervision of Art and Design: Leslie Bauman
Maps: Susan Johnston Carlson

Consultants: Jessie B. Gladden, Divisional Specialist, Office of Social Studies, Baltimore City Schools; Arnold Markoe, Professor, Brooklyn College, City University of New York.

Published by Silver Burdett Press, Inc., a division of Simon & Schuster, Inc., Prentice Hall Building, Englewood Cliffs, NJ 07632.

Library of Congress Cataloging-in-Publication Data
Bennett, Barbara J.
    Stonewall Jackson : Lee's greatest lieutenant / by Barbara J. Bennett : with an introduction by Henry Steele Commager.
        p.   cm. — (The History of the Civil War)
    Includes bibliographical references.
    Summary: A biography of the Confederate general who gained the nickname Stonewall for his stand at the first battle of Bull Run during the Civil War.
    1. Jackson, Stonewall, 1824–1863—Juvenile literature.
2. Generals—United States—Biography—Juvenile literature.
3. United States—History—Civil War, 1861–1865—Campaigns—Juvenile literature.   4. Confederate States of America.   Army—Biography—Juvenile literature. 5. United States.   Army—Biography—Juvenile literature.   [1. Jackson, Stonewall, 1824–1863. 2. Generals.
3. United States—History—Civil War, 1861–1865.]   I. Title.
II. Series.
E467.1.J15B46   1990
973.7′3′092—dc20
[B]
[92]   90-8532
ISBN 0-382-09939-7 (lib. bdg.)   ISBN 0-382-24048-0 (pbk.)   CIP
                                                                                            AC

TABLE OF CONTENTS

Thomas Jonathan Jackson graduated from the U.S. Military Academy at West Point in 1846—just in time to take part in the Mexican-American War. There he had his first experience under fire, and there also he learned the meaning of command. After the war, Jackson took a teaching post at the Virginia Military Institute in Lexington, Virginia. His formal professorship was artillery and philosophy—not a very compatible combination.

Jackson's loyalty was clearly to the South, and when that part of the country seceded in what would become America's great Civil War, he was faced with the problem of which side to fight on. As an officer in the army, Jackson owed his professional loyalty to the Union. As a Southerner, however, his personal loyalty was to the Confederacy. Jackson's personal loyalty won out.

Jackson won fame—and a nickname—early in the war, at the first battle of Bull Run. When the Union troops advanced toward the Confederate lines, Jackson's companies stood their ground, and so did Jackson himself, quite literally. It was in admiration of the stance that an officer from another regiment called out to his own troops, "There stands Jackson like a stone wall." It was a title he bore proudly the rest of his short life.

General Robert E. Lee had great confidence in Jackson. He sent him immediately to the strategically crucial Shenandoah Valley to rout the Federal troops who hoped to detach western Virginia from that state, and to strike for the Confederate capital of Richmond.

Fighting against heavy odds, Jackson conducted one of the most brilliant campaigns in military history, routing two Union armies. Jackson won the admiration of Lee and of the Confederate president, Jefferson Davis. He also won the affection of his troops.

Jackson continued to fight under Lee during the successive campaigns in which Lee out-maneuvered the Yankees—or the Yankee generals, anyway. The critical battle in Lee's Virginia campaign was at Chancellorsville, where the Confederates faced overwhelming odds. In the course of that battle Jackson was struck—accidentally—by a Confederate bullet. A devout Christian who never missed a chance to pray, and whose two wives were both daughters of Presbyterian ministers—Jackson died as courageously as he had lived. He was, next to Lee himself, probably the most beloved of Confederate generals and became—again, after Lee—the one best remembered and most highly esteemed. Both for his courage and for his talents as commanding general, a sympathetic biographer called him "an iron sabre wed to an iron lord."

CIVIL WAR TIME LINE

May 22
Kansas-Nebraska Act states that in new territories the question of slavery will be decided by the citizens. Many Northerners are outraged because this act could lead to the extension of slavery.

| 1854 | 1855 | 1856 | 1857 |

May 21
Lawrence, Kansas is sacked by proslavery Missourians.

May 22
Senator Charles Sumner is caned by Preston Brooks for delivering a speech against slavery.

May 24 – 25
Pottawatomie Creek massacre committed by John Brown and four of his sons.

March 6
The Supreme Court, in the *Dred Scott* ruling, declares that blacks are not U. S. citizens, and therefore cannot bring lawsuits. The ruling divides the country on the question of the legal status of blacks.

January 9 – February 1
Mississippi, Florida, Alabama, Georgia, Louisiana, and Texas secede.

February 4
Seceded states meet to form a new government, the Confederate States of America.

April 13
Fort Sumter, South Carolina, surrenders to Confederacy as Civil War begins.

May 6 – 23
Arkansas, North Carolina, Virginia, and Tennessee secede.

July 21
First Battle of Bull Run/Manassas is won by Confederacy.

July 25
Crittenden Resolution is passed, stating that the purpose of the war is to keep the Union together, not to abolish slavery.

August 6
Confiscation Act is passed, allowing Union to seize property, including slaves, if used in the fight against the Union.

November 6
Jefferson Davis and Alexander Stephens are elected Confederate president and vice president.

October 16
Abolitionist John Brown leads a raid on Harpers Ferry, Virginia, causing Southerners to fear further attacks from the North.

| 1858 | 1859 | 1860 | 1861 |

November 6
Abraham Lincoln is elected president.

December 20
South Carolina secedes from the Union.

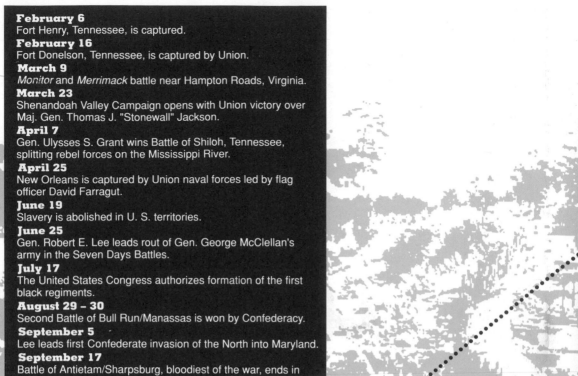

February 6
Fort Henry, Tennessee, is captured.

February 16
Fort Donelson, Tennessee, is captured by Union.

March 9
Monitor and *Merrimack* battle near Hampton Roads, Virginia.

March 23
Shenandoah Valley Campaign opens with Union victory over Maj. Gen. Thomas J. "Stonewall" Jackson.

April 7
Gen. Ulysses S. Grant wins Battle of Shiloh, Tennessee, splitting rebel forces on the Mississippi River.

April 25
New Orleans is captured by Union naval forces led by flag officer David Farragut.

June 19
Slavery is abolished in U. S. territories.

June 25
Gen. Robert E. Lee leads rout of Gen. George McClellan's army in the Seven Days Battles.

July 17
The United States Congress authorizes formation of the first black regiments.

August 29 – 30
Second Battle of Bull Run/Manassas is won by Confederacy.

September 5
Lee leads first Confederate invasion of the North into Maryland.

September 17
Battle of Antietam/Sharpsburg, bloodiest of the war, ends in a stalemate between Lee and McClellan.

1862   **1863**   **1864**   **1865**

January 1
Lincoln issues Emancipation Proclamation, freeing slaves in Confederate states.

March 3
U.S. Congress passes its first military draft.

April 2
Bread riots occur in Richmond, Virginia.

May 1 – 4
Battle of Chancellorsville is won by Confederacy; Stonewall Jackson is accidentally shot by his own troops.

May 22 – July 4
Union wins siege of Vicksburg in Mississippi.

June 3
Lee invades the North from Fredericksburg, Virginia.

July 3
Battle of Gettysburg is won in Pennsylvania by Union.

July 13 – 17
Riots occur in New York City over the draft.

November 19
Lincoln delivers the Gettysburg Address.

March 12
Grant becomes general-in-chief of Union army.

May 5 – 6
Lee and Lt. Gen. James Longstreet defeat Grant at the Wilderness Battle in Virginia.

May 6 – September 2
Atlanta Campaign ends in Union general William Tecumseh Sherman's occupation of Atlanta.

May 8 – 19
Lee and Grant maneuver for position in the Spotsylvania Campaign.

June 3
Grant is repelled at Cold Harbor, Virginia.

June 18, 1864 – April 2, 1865
Grant conducts the Siege of Petersburg, in Virginia, ending with evacuation of the city and Confederate withdrawal from Richmond.

August 5
Admiral Farragut wins Battle of Mobile Bay for Union.

October 6
Union general Philip Sheridan lays waste to Shenandoah Valley, Virginia, cutting off Confederacy's food supplies.

November 8
Lincoln is reelected president.

November 15 – December 13
Sherman's March to the Sea ends with Union occupation of Savannah, Georgia.

March 2
First Reconstruction Act is passed, reorganizing governments of Southern states.

1866	1867	1868	1869

April 9
Civil Rights Act of 1866 is passed. Among other things, it removes states' power to keep former slaves from testifying in court or owning property.

November 3
Ulysses S. Grant is elected president.

January 31
Thirteenth Amendment, freeing slaves, is passed by Congress and sent to states for ratification.

February 1 – April 26
Sherman invades the Carolinas.

February 6
Lee is appointed general-in-chief of Confederate armies.

March 3
Freedman's Bureau is established to assist former slaves.

April 9
Lee surrenders to Grant at Appomattox Courthouse, Virginia.

April 15
Lincoln dies from assassin's bullet, Andrew Johnson becomes president.

May 26
Remaining Confederate troops surrender.

MOUNTAIN BOY

"A youth...of indomitable will and undoubted
courage..."

A TEACHER, ABOUT JACKSON

Seven-year-old Tom Jackson had run away and was hiding deep in the woods. A stranger—an uncle he had never seen—had arrived in the tiny settlement in the western Virginia mountains, and Tom's mother had told him that the stranger would take him and his little sister Laura to live with their grandmother 100 miles across the mountains and to the north.

When Tom was three years old, his father and his older sister Elizabeth had died of typhoid fever. Since then, his mother had worked hard, teaching in the little community's schoolhouse and sewing for her neighbors so that she could take care of the three children who were left to her. These were Tom, his brother Warren, who was three years older, and his sister Laura, who had been born the day after Tom's father died.

Then, a few months before Tom's seventh birthday, his mother had remarried. Soon thereafter, she had sent Warren to live with her brother, Alfred Neale, who lived in Parkersburg, Virginia, which was farther west on the Ohio River. The new little family had then moved from Clarksburg, Virginia, where Tom was born, farther south.

However, Tom's mother was not well enough to take care of even Tom and Laura. And, although Tom's stepfather worked as a lawyer, the family did not have very much money. It was decided that the children must go to live with their father's family in Jackson's Mill, Virginia, on the Monongahela River. Tom loved his mother and did not want to be separated from her. As stubborn and fearless as the general he would grow up to be, Tom ran away to the woods.

That evening, worn out, Tom returned home. For two days, he and Laura listened to the pleadings—and tempting promises—of their uncle and their mother. Finally, they agreed to go.

As it turned out, Tom and Laura were happy in their new home. Their grandmother and her large family of sons and daughters, the children's uncles and aunts, all lived together. They all adored Tom and Laura.

The children had been in Jackson's Mill for only a few weeks when they were told that their mother had given birth to a new baby and was very sick. She wanted to see Tom and Laura before she died. So again they made that long, and this time much sadder, journey. Tom never talked about what his mother said to him before she died, or about how he felt when he lost her. But her wisdom and her prayers to God to protect her children made a deep impression on him. They helped to create in him a strong feeling of religious faith and a sense of right and wrong. Both of these would form his character as a man.

For more than four years, Tom and his sister lived happily with their father's family in Jackson's Mill. There they learned about the family's proud history. Tom's great-grandfather John Jackson had been a tough and stubborn Scotch-Irishman. He had come to America in 1748 from Londonderry in Ulster, Ireland, where President Andrew Jackson's ancestors had also lived. John Jackson settled in the rich mountain wilderness of western Virginia, where the Potomac and James rivers begin their trip to the Atlantic Ocean. He staked a "tomahawk claim" to his lands by cutting marks with his axe into the barks of huge forest trees to show the boundaries of the land he was claiming.

Life in America was not easy for him in the beginning. He lost his first crop of corn to the buffalo, which were still plentiful in

Virginia. He also had to defend himself and his family against the Native Americans who were protecting their hunting grounds from the white settlers.

In time, John Jackson and his eight children prospered. They profited not only from their lands, but also from the mills they had built to cut trees into lumber and to grind corn and other crops for food.

The Jacksons also became important citizens of a new nation. When the American Revolution came, this rich colonist and his sons earned fame and honor fighting for freedom from England.

They married into other well-settled families and held many important public offices in the new nation and in Virginia. One of John Jackson's sons was elected to the new American Congress. One of his grandsons became a federal judge and married the sister of President James Madison's wife, Dolley. Another of John Jackson's sons, Tom's grandfather Edward, settled in Jackson's Mill. Edward became a wealthy landowner and merchant. He went on to represent his county in the Virginia assembly. His son, Tom's father Jonathan, was a wealthy man as well. He practiced law in Clarksburg.

Tom's mother, Julia Neale, also came from an Irish family. The Neales had settled in America long before John Jackson had. Tom was named after Julia's father, Thomas Neale. (Tom would later add the middle name Jonathan to honor his father—and to make his student days at West Point Military Academy less confusing, for another cadet also was named Thomas Jackson.)

Tom's father was a generous man. Perhaps he was too generous, for he used all of his money and his property to help people. At that time, there were no banks that could lend money to people who wanted to open businesses or to build up their farms. Instead, people asked their wealthy neighbors for help. Many people came to Tom's father. He always said yes. But when he died his family was left penniless.

Although both the Neale and the Jackson families helped Julia when she became a widow, she lost many possessions—even the family's pleasant brick cottage on Main Street in Clarksburg. It was sold to pay the debts that Tom's father had left. In the end, friends of Tom's father provided the family with a little one-room house in which to live.

Now, in 1832, the children were orphans living with their relatives. The bright, agreeable Tom became a favorite of his uncle Cummins at Jackson's Mill. Tom helped his uncle with the crops and with caring for the horses. For fun, Tom's uncle took him on fox hunts in the forest and fishing in the Monongahela River.

The people in the little town of Weston near Jackson's Mill used to tell a story about young Tom. Tom made a business deal with Conrad Kester, the local gunsmith to furnish him with fish no smaller than a certain size for 50 cents each. One day, as Tom was taking a handsome three-foot-long pike to Kester, a neighbor stopped him and offered him $1.00 for the fish. Tom told him the fish was sold, but the neighbor insisted that he would pay $1.25, saying Kester surely would not give him more than that. Tom refused, explaining that he had an agreement with Mr. Kester to furnish him fish of a certain length for 50 cents each. He said Kester had taken some fish from him a little shorter than that, and that now he was going to get this big fish for 50 cents.

Tom's strong sense of fair play also made him protective of anyone who was mistreated. On the way to school one day, he saw a big bully insult two girls. Tom immediately attacked the bully and managed to give him a good beating.

Tom was shy, courteous, and serious-minded, but he knew how to have fun, too. He joined in when everyone got together for a house-raising—that is, when they worked together to build a house for a neighbor. He watched with excitement when the strong men would roll freshly cut tree trunks down to the river to float them to the sawmills. Tom's popular uncle Cummins particularly liked to go to the horse races, and Tom loved to go along.

In Jackson's Mill, Tom attended a one-room country school with windowpanes made of greased paper and benches made of split logs. School was open for only three months, during the winter, so that the young people could work on the farms during the rest of the year. One year, Tom attended school for only 39 days. Another year, he was able to go for only two months.

Still, here he was taught reading, spelling, the rules of English grammar, the art of clear and attractive handwriting, basic arithmetic and some mathematics, a little geography, and some history.

Tom did not learn easily, but he kept going over the lessons until he had mastered them. One of his teachers later wrote:

He was a youth of...indomitable will and undoubted courage. He was not what is nowadays termed brilliant, but he was one of those untiring, matter-of-fact persons who would never give up when he engaged in an undertaking until he accomplished his object. He learned slowly, but when he got learning into his head, he never forgot it. He was not quick to decide,...and...then when he made up his mind to do a thing, he did it on short notice and in quick time.

Tom developed a great ambition for more education.

Meanwhile, his uncle Cummins kept him busy outside of school. Cummins, who was considered very sophisticated, had Tom riding his horses as jockey during the races—although Tom was never very good at that. He made Tom a sort of junior partner in his work. Young Tom was sent into the forest in charge of a work crew to cut timber for the mill. He worked with the millers feeding the gristmill. He tended the sheep, beat and reaped the flax crop, and as often as he could, went hunting and fishing.

The autumn Tom was 12 years old, his older brother Warren came to visit. Warren had become a schoolmaster. Tom adored him. Uncle Cummins gave Tom permission to go with his brother to visit their sister Laura, who had gone to live with their uncle Alfred Neale. The Neales lived on a beautiful island in the Ohio River, near Parkersburg in western Virginia. There the boys learned that Alfred Neale and his brother had *bought* the island. They had paid for the land and for clearing off the trees so they could plant crops, by selling the wood from the trees to steamboats on the river to use for fuel.

Tom and Warren thought this was a wonderful way to make their own place in the world. They decided to go on down the Ohio River to find their fortunes.

They built a canoe of logs and went all the way down the Ohio River to the southwest corner of Kentucky, and even on to the Mississippi River. They did not return to Parkersburg until February. During that time, they shared experiences and hardships that they would not talk about when they returned. Instead of making their fortunes, they both had become ill from the cold, windy winter on the rivers. Warren would die three years later of tuberculosis. Tom recovered and walked all the way back to his uncle Cummins's house at Jackson's Mill.

This adventure gave Tom much experience of the world. When he turned 14, he was grown up enough to get a job helping to build a main road for stagecoaches between Staunton in central Virginia and Parkersburg at the state's westernmost point. In this work, he learned about the terrain—the physical features of the land—and how to use engineering tools to build roads. This knowledge was important to Tom later, when he was a general in charge of moving a huge army through the mountains of Virginia.

Tom was also serious about studying the Bible, and was happy to have a talk about religious matters with anyone who was interested. He lent his Bible to one of his best friends, Joe Lightburn, in exchange for Joe's copy of the biography of the "Swamp Fox" Francis Marion, a famous general of the American Revolution. Joe went on to become a Baptist minister, and Tom considered entering the ministry himself. In the Civil War, Joe would fight as a Union general and Tom as a Confederate general.

Tom continued to go to school, and even taught some pupils himself, but he struggled with the lessons. Still, the more he taught, the more he wanted to go to college, where a man could learn "how to work his head," he said.

When Tom was 17, he was elected a constable of his county. It was a difficult and often unpleasant job collecting small overdue debts. An older, more mature man had been considered necessary for such a responsibility. But Tom's uncle Cummins supported him for the job. He never regretted it. Tom had the good judgment, self-reliance, and shrewdness that were required.

Once a poor woman asked Tom to collect a debt from a man who refused to pay what he owed her. The man began avoiding

Tom. Finally, Tom decided to make a claim on the man's horse to force him to pay his debt. The horse was the man's most important personal property because without it he could not conduct his business. However, the law said that the horse could not be seized when its owner was in the saddle.

Tom figured out how to get the horse. He hid outside the stable, and when the man rode up and dismounted, Tom grabbed the reins. The man jumped back into the saddle and began lashing at Tom with his whip. But Tom held tight to the reins and led the horse toward the stable door. When they got to the low doorway, the man had to dismount so he would not hit his head on the doorway and be badly hurt. Tom had possession of the horse, and the man was forced to pay his debt before he could get his horse back.

This job taught Tom that he was able to do whatever he was determined to do. It demonstrated to the people of the county that to him, his oath of office was a solemn obligation to be fulfilled to the letter. Tom was someone who was true to his word. His good will and his record of honesty with the people of the county helped him toward something he wanted more than anything else in the world—a college education.

TOM JACKSON, CADET

"You may be whatever you resolve to be."

THOMAS JACKSON

Tom was close to reaching his fondest dream—a real education. There was a chance that he might get an appointment to the United States Military Academy at West Point. It would mean that even though he had no money, he would receive four years of the finest education available. At the same time, he would be trained for the honorable career of an officer in the military service of the country.

Then, as now, appointments to West Point were made through the recommendation of the member of Congress for the district where the young man lived. Many young men were eager to be selected as cadets at West Point, and that year, 1842, there were four in Tom's district who wanted the appointment. Tom, his friend Joe Lightburn, Gibson Butcher, and Johnson Camden all stepped forward, so an examination was held to help Congressman Samuel L. Hays make a choice.

When Tom failed the mathematics section and Gibson Butcher got the appointment, it seemed Tom's dream was over. But one day a few weeks after this disappointment, Uncle Cummins took his horse to the blacksmith for new shoes, and learned that Butcher had come home. He had discovered that life at West Point was nothing but schedules and discipline and drilling and saluting and tough studying. Unable to stand it, he had simply quit.

Uncle Cummins and Tom immediately set to work to have him chosen to fill that vacancy. Many of the people in the district who knew of Tom's seriousness and honesty joined in a letter to Congressman Hays asking him to support Tom's application. When one lawyer in the community asked Tom if he were not afraid that his education was too poor to let him be successful at West Point, Tom replied: "I am very ignorant but I can make it up in study. I know I have the energy and I think I have the intellect. At least, I am determined to try, and I want you to help me." The lawyer wrote a special letter of commendation to Congressman Hays, mentioning especially Tom's courage and determination.

Tom then worked with a friend, another lawyer, to prepare for the entrance examination at West Point, which he would face if Hays selected him. Finally, he received word that Hays would support him. Tom immediately packed his saddlebags and left for Washington, D.C. He rode his horse hard in order to catch the stagecoach in Clarksburg, but he missed it. So he simply spurred his horse on to catch the coach at its next stop.

When Tom got to Washington, he went straight to Congressman Hays's office. After a talk, the congressman took Tom to Secretary of War John C. Spencer, who grilled the young applicant. An eyewitness said that Tom responded "with the grit of Old Hickory" (President Andrew Jackson's nickname), and he showed so much "manliness and resolution" that Secretary Spencer said to him, "Sir, you have a good name. Go to West Point, and the first man who insults you knock him down, and have it charged to my account!"

Tom left for New York City. From there he went by boat up the Hudson River to West Point. He arrived on June 20, 1842.

What Tom saw was awesome. It was a mammoth gray stone fortress, built high on a cliff over an S-curve in New York State's Hudson River. This was the fortress that the traitor Benedict Arnold had plotted to give, for money, to the enemy British during the American revolution.

Tom knew West Point would be a tough place to be successful. He squared his shoulders and stalked into his barracks.

He seemed a funny figure to his new classmates. He was about 5 feet 10 inches tall, with a high forehead, a small, grim mouth, a ruddy farmer's complexion, a mop of brown hair, and monstrously large feet. Most amusing of all to the other cadets, many of whom came from the wealthy eastern college towns, were his clothes. Tom wore a large, coarse, black felt hat (a leftover from his days as a constable), gray homespun clothing, and huge muddy boots. He was all angles and walked clumsily, moving fast with his upper body bent forward. A little group of cadets watched him, among them two future Confederate generals, A. P. Hill and Dabney H. Maury. Tom looked so determined that one of them said, "That fellow looks as if he has come to stay."

Tom was indeed intent on succeeding at West Point. He wrote a journal of rules for self-improvement. Among them were:

Sacrifice your life rather than your word.
You may be whatever you resolve to be.

First, Tom sat for the entrance examination—and passed it. But then he had to survive the famous "plebe summer": The freshman cadets were sent out to camp on the huge plain near the academy until the end of August. They learned "soldierly bearing," personal discipline, and how to drill. They slept on the bare ground during heat and rain. It was a rugged introduction to his next four years, and Tom suffered greatly from homesickness. He missed his sister Laura and Uncle Cummins and Jackson's Mill.

Tom's poor earlier schooling and his slowness in learning made just staying in school a victory. The first year he was one of "the immortals," a nickname for those whose grades were the lowest in their class. Of 72 students, he was 70th in French, 45th in mathematics, which included algebra and geometry, and 51st in general merit. He got 15 demerits, penalties given for poor conduct and performance apart from the cadet's schoolwork. Tom's demerits were for such faults as a poorly cleaned musket or badly polished boots.

Tom studied long past "lights out." He would fill the fire grate with a load of coal and lie beside it full length on the floor, working late into the night. He would sit bolt upright at his study table and stare hard at the wall or at the ceiling, reviewing and memorizing the lessons. This ability to concentrate on the subject at hand and to remember would help him later, when he became a military leader.

Tom was not easily discouraged. Neither low grades, nor what his classmates thought of him, nor the discipline of West Point would keep him from reaching his goal. His book of rules would help him:

Disregard public opinion when it interferes with your duty.
Avoid trifling conversation.
Lose no time; be always employed in something useful.
It is not desirable to have a large number of intimate friends... If
   you have *one* who is what he should be, you are... happy.

Highlights in the Life of Stonewall Jackson

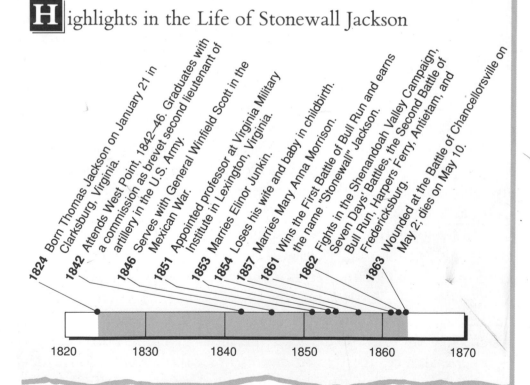

1824 Born Thomas Jackson on January 21 in Clarksburg, Virginia.

1842 Attends West Point, 1842–46. Graduates with a commission as brevet second lieutenant of artillery in the U.S. Army.

1846 Serves with General Winfield Scott in the Mexican War.

1851 Appointed professor at Virginia Military Institute in Lexington, Virginia.

1853 Marries Elinor Junkin.

1854 Loses his wife and baby in childbirth.

1857 Marries Mary Anna Morrison.

1861 Wins the First Battle of Bull Run and earns the name "Stonewall" Jackson.

1862 Fights in the Shenandoah Valley Campaign, Seven Days' Battles, the Second Battle of Bull Run, Harpers Ferry, Antietam, and Fredericksburg.

1863 Wounded at the Battle of Chancellorsville on May 2; dies on May 10.

1820   1830   1840   1850   1860   1870

In spite of his seriousness, Tom had a reputation for personal warmth and kindness. When something interested him, one observer wrote, "His form became erect, his eyes flashed like steel, and a smile, as sweet as a woman's, would illumine his whole face."

If someone were sick or had received bad news from home, Tom could be counted on to be especially kind and sympathetic. He was very sensitive to death. When a cadet was accidentally drowned, Tom wrote to Laura about it: "The news must have inflicted a sore wound on the hearts of his parents."

After his second year, Tom was chosen by his fellow cadets to be a student officer. One cadet later wrote:

> While there were many who seemed to surpass him in...geniality [cheerfulness], and in good-fellowship, there was no one of our class who more absolutely possessed the respect and confidence of all; and in the end "Old Jack" as he was always called, with his...earnestness, his...straightforwardness, and his high sense of honour, came to be regarded by his comrades with something very like affection.

Tom's school record showed steady improvement. He was among the lowest in his class the first year. By the time the class graduated in 1846, Tom was ranked 12th in engineering, 5th in ethics, 11th in artillery, and 11th in mineralogy and geology, and he had only seven demerits for the year. His lowest rank was in infantry tactics: 21st. Twelve cadets had dropped out by the final year. In the remaining class of 60, there was the future Union general George McClellan and the future Confederate general George Pickett (who was at the bottom of the class). Tom stood seventeenth in graduating rank, solidly in the top third of the class.

The cadets joked that it was too bad that West Point did not last *five* years—by then "Old Tom" would have been number one in his class!

Because of his good standing, Tom could choose which branch of the army he wanted to join. He chose the artillery, where he was given the rank of brevet second lieutenant. (As a *brevet* second lieutenant, he had the honorary title of an officer, but his salary would be lower.)

The artillery had been the choice of the brilliant French general Napoleon Bonaparte. Young Lieutenant Jackson had chosen well.

THE MEXICAN WAR

"I should like to be in one battle."

THOMAS JACKSON

or years, many people in the United States had wanted their country to reach all the way across the vast North American continent to the Pacific Ocean. The nation almost doubled in size in 1803, when President Thomas Jefferson purchased the territory of Louisiana—many times the size of today's state of Louisiana—from the French. By 1845, many Americans were saying that it was obviously the fate, the "manifest destiny," of the country to include all of the land across the West to the Pacific.

Thousands of settlers from the United States went West. Some went by sea, sailing around the tip of South America to California. Others crossed the wilderness on the exhausting and dangerous overland trails.

But much of this western land did not belong to the United States. In the 1820s, settlers from the United States had arrived on the rich plains of Texas, a part of Mexico. At first, the Mexican government welcomed them and gave them free land so that they would stay and plant valuable crops of cotton. President John Quincy Adams and then President Andrew Jackson offered to buy Texas, but Mexico refused to sell.

The Mexican government was afraid it would lose Texas because almost all of the settlers were from the United States and preferred their own religion and way of life. For example, Mexican law required that all immigrants be Catholic, while the Americans desired to choose their own faith, most often Protestant. Many settlers brought slaves with them. Mexico outlawed slavery, so the settlers evaded the law by "freeing" their slaves and then forcing them to sign contracts for a lifetime of work. Finally, in 1830, Mexico refused to allow in any more settlers from the United States.

Meanwhile, the Texans had become wealthy and powerful, and they wanted their independence from Mexico. In 1835, they rebelled. In 1836, the fearsome Mexican general Santa Anna attacked the Texans in their fort at San Antonio, an old stone Spanish mission called the Alamo. There were only 187 Texans, among them Davy Crockett, the famous frontiersman, and Jim Bowie, the inventor of the Bowie knife. They held off the Mexican army of 6,000 men for about 10 days. Finally, the Mexicans got into the fort and killed everyone, soaking the corpses in oil and burning them.

Then Sam Houston, a great military leader, reorganized the rebels' army and defeated General Santa Anna at the Battle of San Jacinto, just about six weeks after the battle at the Alamo. Santa Anna was forced to recognize Texan independence. Houston was elected president of the new Republic of Texas. At once the Texans asked to become part of the United States.

The Americans argued for nine years about whether to annex Texas. The nation's desire to increase its size helped to settle the issue. In 1845, Texas became part of the Union. Mexico promptly severed relations with the United States.

A boundary dispute followed. The United States said that Texas stretched as far south as the Rio Grande. The Mexican government said that its border was farther north, at the Nueces River. President James K. Polk sent General Zachary Taylor ("Old Rough and Ready" to his soldiers) into the disputed area with 1,500 troops. At the same time, the president tried to settle the dispute over the

Sam Houston, hero of San Jacinto, went on to become president of the Republic of Texas.

boundary with an offer of money to Mexico. He also tried to purchase the lands of California and the huge New Mexico territory.

But the Mexicans refused even to consider negotiations. The president sent General Taylor (who later would be elected president of the United States), with a 4,000-man army to the northern bank of the Rio Grande. The Mexicans sent a small force across the river. It attacked an American horse patrol. This small skirmish was President Polk's excuse to send a war message to Congress, saying the Mexicans had "shed American blood on American soil... War exists..."

A young American lieutenant, Ulysses S. Grant (later a Civil War general and president of the United States), afterward called the Mexican War "one of the most unjust ever waged by a stronger against a weaker nation." In this conflict, Americans from both Northern and Southern states fought side by side and learned the techniques of waging war. Later they would use their experience to fight against each other when the terrible Civil War tore their country apart.

President Polk had a war plan to get from Mexico what the Americans wanted. First of all, the Mexicans would be pushed out of Texas altogether. Next, the Americans would invade and occupy northern Mexico, seize California and New Mexico, and then march on to Mexico City and occupy the nation's capital.

Thomas Jackson did not want to miss this war, but he had to wait patiently for his military orders. After he graduated from West Point, he went to visit his sister Laura and his uncle Cummins in Virginia. There the country was gripped by war fever. Right away, Jackson was asked to help raise and drill a company of volunteers for the Mexican War.

Finally, Jackson's orders arrived. He left immediately to join his artillery company at Fort Hamilton, New York. The men marched 400 miles overland to Pittsburgh, Pennsylvania. There they took a steamboat down the Ohio and Mississippi rivers to New Orleans. Finally, they sailed to join General Taylor at Point Isabel in Texas.

Disappointment awaited Jackson at Point Isabel. He learned that General Taylor had moved south toward Mexico City, and had fought and captured the town of Monterrey. An eight-week armistice had been declared. When Jackson met Lieutenant Daniel Harvey Hill, who was also a West Point graduate (and would later become Jackson's brother-in-law and serve on his staff during the Civil War), Tom told him, "I really envy you men who have been in action. I should like to be in one battle."

For six long months, the eager lieutenant was kept on boring garrison duty—he had to stay at the army post set up at Point Isabel. He acted as company supply officer and installed guns to defend the barren point. Finally, he was sent with the occupation force to the Mexican town of Saltillo. The men were awaiting orders for an overland assault on Mexico City.

However, the distance from Saltillo to the capital city was more than 600 miles through rough, mountainous, unfriendly country. The army needed another plan, so it turned to old General Winfield Scott, a veteran of the War of 1812 and a genius at war planning. Scott took charge of a style of warfare that had never been tried before. He was to make an "amphibious" assault: combine the army and navy forces and attack the enemy by sea. They would land at Veracruz, Mexico's major seaport and fortress on the Gulf of Mexico. From there, they would make a shorter overland march of 260 miles to Mexico City. Scott would use the National Road, which the Spanish conqueror Cortes had followed when he invaded Mexico more than 300 years earlier.

Tom Jackson's unit was taken away from the northern army of occupation and sent to join Scott's assault on Mexico City.

After General Santa Anna's defeat by Sam Houston in 1836, he had gone into exile in Cuba. But he was now the president of Mexico and in charge of its defense. President Polk had brought him back to Mexico after he promised Polk that he would grant the Americans the kind of treaty they wanted. However, the other Mexican leaders had been outraged at the American demands, so Santa Anna had yet to grant the treaty.

Santa Anna heard that the American troops were being withdrawn from the Rio Grande. Figuring he could wipe out the Americans remaining there and still keep General Scott from seizing the port of Veracruz, the Mexican general marched north.

General Scott found Veracruz an easy target. He took his army of 13,000 men, with all its weapons and supplies, on board a huge fleet of ships. They landed on a beach just outside the range of the cannon at the city's fortress, the Castle of San Juan de Ulua. Jackson, as an officer in the First Artillery, led an assault boat of soldiers and commanded a battery of powerful guns. He proudly wrote his sister, "A cannon ball came in about five steps of me."

The city of Veracruz fell easily. It was defended by only 4,000 men, and the Americans' heavier cannon and greater numbers made the amphibious assault a great victory. Jackson was promoted to first lieutenant "for gallant and meritorious conduct at the siege of Vera Cruz."

The Americans permitted the Mexican defenders to withdraw and retreat, a common custom of warfare in those days. Jackson wrote Laura, "I approve of all except allowing the enemy to retire; that I cannot approve of, . . . as we . . . could have taken them prisoners of. war unconditionally." This became one of Jackson's rules of good generalship: He felt it was senseless to allow the enemy soldiers to go free, because they could then rejoin their army and go on fighting.

Then the American forces began their march to Mexico City, along the National Road. Their next step in the Mexican War was to capture this important central city.

But the long march there was not an easy one. The men suffered from diarrhea and were fearful because it was the yellow fever season. They took their guns and wagons over the decaying road, higher and higher into the mountains. Jackson saw a riot of color in the "wilderness of trees and flowers." But as they moved along, the men searched anxiously for an ambush from Mexican soldiers defending their homeland.

On a high, cone-shaped hill named Cerro Gordo, they found General Santa Anna and the enemy soldiers entrenched with heavy guns on either side of the National Road. Two young captains in the engineer corps, Robert E. Lee and George McClellan, were sent out to scout for a road behind the enemy soldiers that the Americans could use. They did not find one, but they saw a path through the rough terrain. They hacked a road through, attacked the Mexican soldiers, and when they began to retreat, pursued them.

On Cerro Gordo, Jackson learned two important lessons about battle that later became his trademark. The first was to scout—that is, to get information about the enemy and his positions. The second was to flank—that is, to move around the enemy rather than attack directly. Finally, he learned the importance of pursuing a retreating enemy and capturing him.

Next, Jackson got assigned to a tough light artillery unit under the command of the hot-tempered, unpopular Captain John Magruder. Jackson had learned about the value of light artillery—it was easy to move around quickly in the thick of battle—and he believed that this dangerous assignment would lead to honor and fame.

Jackson saw some action even before he joined the unit. On his way to join the unit, a large band of Mexican guerrillas attacked Jackson and his escorts. It became a desperate hand-to-hand fight, and Jackson killed four guerrillas, took three prisoners, and took for himself a beautiful Mexican sword, a saber that he later gave to his adoring nephew, Laura's son, Thomas Arnold Jackson. Jackson had finally fought and had the experience of killing in battle.

The American army's finest officers fought in the campaign for Mexico City. General Franklin Pierce, later elected president of the United States, helped Scott in his assault; Robert E. Lee was on Scott's staff. Many future Civil War generals were young officers and learned the arts of war firsthand in Mexico. D. H. Hill, "Jube" Early, Joe Johnston, James Longstreet, Pierre G. T. Beauregard, Dick Ewell, George Pickett, and Barnard Bee would later fight alongside Jackson for the Confederacy. Ulysses S. Grant, Joe Hooker, William Tecumseh Sherman, George McClellan, George Meade, and Irvin McDowell would fight for the Union.

As the U.S. Army approached Mexico City, General Scott sent Captain Lee out to discover a way to cross the forbidding wasteland that lay before the city. Lee found a mule path, but his men had to widen the path so that it was big enough to carry the wagons with their cannons. Magruder's men were brought up to the edge of the wasteland, a huge field of hardened lava with deep cracks and sharp rocks. Jackson was put in charge of the guns. The infantry and artillery were pinned down by Mexican shellfire and could not draw near the city without being overrun by Mexican soldiers on horseback. But Jackson's men met the severe Mexican fire and continued the attack "in handsome style, and with equal briskness and effect," Magruder reported. For his "gallant and meritorious conduct," Jackson was promoted to captain.

Now the men were at the very gates of the city, but they had yet to make the toughest assault of all: They had to take over the magnificent castle of Chapultepec. It was a fortress on a high hill, standing guard over the city. It was a symbol of Mexico's power, because it was the home of Mexico's military academy.

General Santa Anna had put 1,000 of his best troops in Chapultepec. The Americans had to assault the stone walls of the fortress. While they brought up their big guns and scaling ladders, their pickaxes and crowbars, the Mexican marksmen poured fire down on them. The American commander was wounded, and his men wavered.

One of Jackson's guns was knocked out, most of his horses were killed, and his men became demoralized. But Jackson stormed up and down in the hail of lead, crying, "There is no danger. See! I am not hit." (Later, he said that was the only lie he had ever told.) Then he had his cannon lifted up and moved across a huge protective ditch, where he proceeded to load, fire, swab, and reload, ignoring the roar from above. When orders came to retreat, Jackson refused. His second gun was working again, so he held his ground and unnerved the Mexicans, while the American troops moved forward and attacked the fortress.

At the end, even the 100 Mexican boy cadets called "Los Niños," the youngest of whom was 13 years old, joined the brave effort to fight off the Americans. They were cut down with the full thrust of the vicious assault. It was no use. Chapultepec, the symbol of national pride and the last defense of the city, fell.

Jackson hitched his guns to wagons and, followed by two other lieutenants, D. H. Hill and Barnard Bee, led the pursuit of the retreating Mexicans toward the city. The Mexicans tried once again, with 1,500 cavalrymen, to stop the Americans. However, Jackson's guns opened fire and tore huge holes in their ranks. They retreated, and the Americans won Mexico City.

Jackson was singled out for his brave fighting in General Scott's reports. He was promoted to major. Captain Magruder said of Jackson, "If devotion, industry, talent and gallantry are the highest qualities of a soldier, then he is entitled to the distinction which their profession confers."

Jackson saw his first military action in the Mexican War.

For nine months Jackson stayed in the beautiful Mexican capital, living in luxurious rooms in the National Palace, having breakfast in bed, and enjoying the leisurely Spanish social life. He studied the Spanish language and had long talks with the Roman Catholic priests in the beautiful cathedrals. In a letter to Laura, he hinted that he might choose to settle down with "some amiable Señorita."

The peaceful months in Mexico City were also a time for some soul-searching. Jackson had serious talks with his good friend Captain Francis Taylor. Taylor asked him how a man like Jackson, who had such a strong sense of right and wrong, could be so casual about church. Why, he did not even know whether he had been baptized! Yet Jackson remembered his mother's prayers for him when she was dying. He now felt a need to join forces with his God, who would help him to control his tremendous ambition and lead a successful life.

The peace treaty, signed in February 1848 at the little village of Guadalupe Hidalgo just outside Mexico City, ended the war. Mexico gave up its claims to its northern lands, including California, where only the month before amazing deposits of gold had been discovered. The United States had won a huge territory, a giant step toward its "manifest destiny" of stretching from the Atlantic to the Pacific Ocean.

Jackson was sent back to the United States. He visited Laura and his nephew, and then he reported for his new assignment at Fort Hamilton in New York.

Here Jackson was baptized a Christian in an Episcopal service, but he decided not to join any church until he had studied more about it. His health was not as good in New York as it had been when he was in a fighting army. He wondered if his ill health was punishment from God for sins he did not know about. He prayed, and he ate only lean meat and stale bread without butter. He would take no tea, coffee, or alcoholic drinks. He once explained, after an experience of drunkenness, "I like the taste of them [alcoholic drinks], and...I made up my mind at once to do without them altogether."

Jackson exercised constantly, taking fast walks and thrusting one of his arms up in the air every few steps because he believed it was heavier than the other arm. He kept to a strict schedule of sleeping and eating. Among his fellow officers, Jackson's reputation for being peculiar grew.

It was not long before Jackson was called to active duty again. The army needed men on the Indian frontier in Florida, where bands of Seminole Indians were fighting the white settlers. Jackson was sent to a desolate fort isolated in marshland, far from any society like that in Mexico City or New York. His duties included leading forays through the swamps against the Native Americans. The American Indians were experts at hiding themselves and at warfare in the swamps, so Jackson was not successful in these missions. Also, he did not get along well with his commander, William Henry French, a fellow soldier from his days in the First Artillery in Mexico.

Then one day in February 1851, Jackson received a letter from the Virginia Military Institute. A teaching position had opened up, and D. H. Hill, another of Jackson's fellow soldiers in Mexico, had recommended him for the job. He was invited to teach natural and experimental philosophy and artillery tactics at the military academy.

Accepting such an offer meant Jackson would have to resign from the army. But it also meant leaving Florida, where he was so unhappy and also so far away from his family. If he accepted the post, he would have a way to support himself outside the army. Also, he would still be called "Major," and he would have the respect due a professor. Jackson decided to accept.

Before he reported for his new job, Jackson decided to seek advice about his health. His eyes were bothering him, and he still had problems with his stomach. A doctor in New York told him that his stomach gave him trouble because of his nerves. Jackson was put on a strict diet that included buttermilk. The doctor told him to exercise, not to work so hard, and to play more. He also said the best medicine of all would be to get married.

Jackson was 27 years old. His life so far had been one of hard work on the frontier, hard studying at West Point, and then hard fighting in a war. He had lived far away from his home and family. He had never really learned how to talk with young women, or how to please them well enough to ask one to be his wife. It was easy to exercise and follow a strict diet—he had always done these things. But to learn to have fun, and to ask a woman to marry him? To Jackson, these were the biggest challenges.

MAJOR JACKSON, THE TEACHER

"This grand, gloomy & peculiarly good man…"

A CADET, ABOUT JACKSON

Lexington, Virginia, was a beautiful town at the foot of the Blue Ridge Mountains, in the rich valley of the Shenandoah River. The name *Shenandoah* came from the American Indian words for "bright daughter of the stars."

For nearly 100 years, Lexington had been the home of Washington College (named for George Washington, who had given much money for its support). Together, the college and the Virginia Military Institute (VMI) gave the town a warm social life. Fitting into this social life proved to be Professor Jackson's biggest problem. He was a soldier, used to rough living. Try as he might, he could not learn the custom of casual visiting.

He did accept some invitations, but the visits were usually painful experiences. He would sit bolt upright, not relaxing enough even to rest his back against the chair. He was extremely polite, but his conversation did not come easily. He was so exact that he would not say anything that was not absolutely correct and honest.

Then he promptly set about making himself very unpopular with the cadets he taught at the Institute. Most of them later remembered their awkward, grim professor sitting motionless in front of the classroom, listening as they recited their lessons. He would correct them and quote long passages from the textbook from memory. If a student asked for more explanation, or another way to understand a problem, Jackson would not provide it. Instead, he would simply repeat the lesson from memory.

Jackson had a naturally humble personality. If a student asked a direct question that he could not answer, Jackson said outright that he did not know the answer. This made many students believe that he was weak and uncertain, so they became disrespectful.

Jackson was very strict about discipline. If a student broke any of the school's rules, his punishment was swift and hard. He even used the court-martial procedure to keep order among the cadets. This meant a board was formed to consider any serious disobedience of the rules, just as in the army. The most severe punishment was to be expelled from the school.

Jackson was so unpopular that he was the butt of cruel pranks. One day some upperclassmen tied a gagged "rat"—their name for a freshman, or first-year student—to a chair, then tilted the chair against Jackson's door, knocked loudly, and ran off. When "Old Jack" opened the door, the "rat" fell at his feet.

Jackson saw to it that the guilty cadets were expelled.

At the same time, Jackson's respect for learning and for correctness led him to make an apology that became a legend at VMI. One day in class he scolded a student for what he thought was an incorrect answer. After he went to bed that night, Jackson realized the answer had been correct. So he dressed and walked through a cold rain to the student's dormitory to offer him an apology. Such behavior earned him the name of "Tom Fool" behind his back. But it also made people realize that to Jackson truth was the most important thing, and that he demanded the best from himself as well as from others.

The cadets who knew him best could appreciate him. His seriousness and strict discipline made Jackson a man to be trusted. One cadet wrote that he had "the extraordinary advantages to learn to honor & to respect...this grand, gloomy & peculiarly *good* man."

Jackson slowly got used to life in Lexington. He became more sociable. He went to all the churches and discussed their various religious teachings. His good friend D. H. Hill gave him the

Presbyterian Church's *Shorter Catechism*, a book of religious teaching. After he had studied it and talked with the minister, Jackson
joined that church. And there he met a young woman who would
change his life.

Elinor Junkin was the daughter of the president of Washington
College, the Reverend Dr. George Junkin. The correct young
officer from VMI took great interest in "Ellie." He became a
constant visitor at the Junkin home and spent a great deal of time in
close conversation with her.

One day while he was talking with D. H. Hill, Jackson said he
could not understand what had come over him. He had known
Ellie for almost two years, and suddenly his feelings toward her
had changed greatly. Hill laughed and said, "You are in love; that's
what is the matter."

Jackson then decided to ask her to marry him. At first Ellie said
no, but in the end she agreed to marry Tom Jackson. Their
engagement was kept secret.

D. H. Hill said the way he kept his wedding plans a secret
showed how he would command in the army in later years. He

never told *anyone* of his plans, which made his army wonder what he was doing. But Jackson's secrecy also was a major reason for his success as a general.

When Tom Jackson and Elinor Junkin were married in August 1853, it was a surprise to everyone. The newlyweds' life together was wonderful. On their honeymoon, they visited New York City, West Point, and Niagara Falls in the United States. They went to Canada to visit Montreal and the Plains of Abraham near Quebec.

When Ellie announced that she was going to have a baby, Jackson felt that his life was complete. Even when the University of Virginia refused to give him a teaching job, he was so happy that it was not hard to accept the bad news. Jackson took Ellie on a vacation trip to Natural Bridge, a few miles south of Lexington, and on a visit to his sister Laura. He felt the trip would be good for her, and she would have plenty of time to rest before the baby came, in October 1854.

But tragedy awaited him. Both Ellie and the baby died in childbirth. Jackson was plunged into grief. He visited the grave site every day. He wanted to die himself and wrote, "Ah, if it only might please God to let me go now!" In an effort to turn his grief into something good, he wrote, "Objects to be effected by Ellie's death: To eradicate ambition; to eradicate resentment; to produce humility. If you desire to be more heavenly-minded, think more of the things of heaven, and less of the things of earth."

Jackson found comfort in his work for the Presbyterian church. He considered the pastor, Dr. William White, to be like a commanding officer. When Dr. White told his congregation what was expected of them as Christians, Jackson took his words as orders and worked hard to fulfill them. When Jackson collected money for the Bible Society, his list of contributors included the names of church members, of course. But penciled at the bottom were also the names of people who had given just a few pennies— the free blacks of Lexington. Jackson had asked for their contributions as well, for the Christian cause.

This gave him an idea. He organized a Sunday school for free African Americans and slaves. This was very hard to do, and he conducted the first meetings alone. But his stubbornness and dedication paid off. He soon had 100 students, the church supported his Sunday school, and he had plenty of volunteers to teach.

When the minister suggested that the church members, including Jackson, should volunteer to lead the prayers in church, Jackson felt this was an order that must be obeyed. But it was a painful duty for him to perform. He felt that he did not know enough about religion, and he hated speaking in public.

Jackson's turn to lead the prayers came, and it was a disaster. He was so sweaty and miserable that everyone was embarrassed for him. Weeks passed, and he was not asked again. When he talked with Dr. White about it, the minister said he felt it was best not to spoil Jackson's pleasure in the church by making him so uncomfortable. Jackson responded that "my comfort or discomfort is not the question; if it is my duty...then I must persevere...until I learn to do it right..." He finally did learn to lead the prayers without suffering.

His grief had eased, but he still missed Ellie. Jackson decided to take a vacation. In the summer of 1856, he took a long trip to Europe, where he saw beautiful cathedrals and famous works of art. He studied the French language and learned it so well that thereafter he began to read his morning Bible lessons in French.

His trip to Europe gave Jackson a new outlook, and by the time he came home, he had decided to remarry. He even had someone in mind—the charming Mary Anna Morrison, the sister-in-law of his close friend D. H. Hill. Hill had left Lexington and was teaching at Davidson College in North Carolina. Jackson remembered the happy times when the Hills had been in Lexington and Mary Anna and her sister had visited.

Now he wrote to Mary Anna in North Carolina. At Christmas he paid an unexpected visit, with the purpose, he told the Morrison family, of courting Mary Anna. Her father considered him "a Christian gentleman," and her mother thought him extremely polite. He returned to his teaching at VMI and courted "Anna" with beautiful letters. Finally, in July 1857, they were married in her father's home.

Their life together in Lexington was happy. Jackson said his home had every door "on golden hinges" because of the peace and good order that prevailed.

Jackson had a daily schedule, and Anna enjoyed helping him to stick to it. He got up at six o'clock every morning, knelt in prayer, took a cold bath, and had a brisk walk. Promptly at seven o'clock, he held prayers for his family and the servants. After his breakfast, he taught at the Institute until 11:00 A.M. Until dinner at 1:00 P.M., he studied—first his Bible, and then his textbooks for the next day's lessons. He would allow no interruptions during his study time. He would stand at a high desk that was made especially for him and memorize the lessons.

The afternoons were given over to buggy rides, often with his wife, out to the large, bountiful farm where he worked on his crops of vegetables and fruit trees. In the evening, he could not read by lamp light because of his weak eyes, but he would stand in absolute concentration facing the wall, again demanding not to be interrupted. He was reviewing the material he had studied in the morning. He loved to have Anna read to him in the evenings. And with Anna he could relax and be playful—the cadets at the Institute would not have recognized him.

They were very happy when Anna became pregnant. But as so often happened at that time, their beautiful baby, a girl, soon died, and the Jacksons were heartbroken.

In their home, Tom and Anna had several slaves. Some were given to Anna by her family, and some Tom had bought. Jackson's attitude was typical of most white Southerners at that time. He did not consider slavery to be evil or a moral wrong. He believed that the Bible taught that it was all right to own slaves. He did feel that the owners of slaves were obligated to care for them and treat them well, and, in addition, to teach them about God and Christianity. He was known for his kindness to all people.

The first slave Jackson bought was named Albert. Albert came to the respected Major Jackson and asked if he would buy him. Albert's plan was to work to repay the cost of the purchase in installments. When the money was repaid, he would be free.

Jackson agreed to the plan. Albert did not live with Jackson, but worked as a waiter in a hotel. Once when Albert became ill, Jackson brought him to his own home and had him nursed back to health.

Another time, an old woman named Amy came to Jackson and begged that he buy her because she was about to be sold away to an unknown master. She was a cook, and Jackson was not yet married and could not use her services. He bought her and arranged for her to work and live with a kind family until he got married and took her to live with him. In 1861, when Jackson went to war and Anna returned to her family in North Carolina, he paid a free African American woman in Lexington to take the aged Amy into her home and care for her. Amy died when he was away at war, and he wrote Anna, "I send you a letter announcing that Amy has gone to a better world. The tears came to my eyes more than once while reading it."

Jackson spent 10 years in Lexington. He was happy with his family and his home, and he was a respected member of his community. But public affairs and a cruel division in the nation were soon to intrude on his happiness and take Jackson away to war.

THE NATION SPLITS IN TWO

"The wind blew his lifeless body to and fro…"
JACKSON, ABOUT JOHN BROWN

By the late 1850s, the peaceful life of the citizens of Lexington, Virginia, was soon to come to an end. Tension had been building throughout the United States, and it would tear the country apart.

Ever since the nation was founded, citizens had been divided over the issue of slavery. Many people, mostly in the Northern states, believed that slavery was evil and that it had no place in a democratic nation. They believed strongly that the practice of men and women owning other men and women was a moral wrong. They also believed the form of slavery practiced in the United States during the 19th century to be the most brutal and inhuman in recorded history.

Most Southerners saw nothing wrong with the institution of slavery. To support their argument, they said that according to the Bible slavery was all right, and that societies throughout history had had slaves.

White Southerners asked the question, What would happen if the four million slaves in the South were all freed? Since Thomas Jefferson's time, emancipation societies had been proposing plans to establish colonies for African Americans in Africa and elsewhere. These plans were generally unsuccessful. So the question remained: How would the huge former slave population fit into the white society?

Many whites in both the North and South believed that if the slaves were freed, they would present a threat to the position of white laborers in the national economy.

Also, when Northerners talked about freeing the slaves, Southerners believed they were encouraging slaves to rise up. They feared bloodshed. There were many areas in the South where slaves outnumbered whites. There had been some slave revolts already. If these ideas were to spread through the South, the whites feared, their lives would be in danger.

Southerners also defended slavery because their wealth depended on slave labor. In 1793, Eli Whitney had invented the cotton gin, a machine that could clean cotton of its seeds. Until that time, this process had been done slowly, by hand. Thereafter, the production of cotton boomed. The plantation owners grew rich selling cotton to be made into cloth in textile factories in the North and in Europe. As their plantations grew, so did their dependence on slaves.

It was not just on the issue of slavery that the regions differed. They had different economic systems, and therefore their interests were often at odds. In the early days, nearly everyone was a farmer. The United States was known as "a nation of small farmers." However, over the years, industry began to develop in the North while large plantations grew in the South.

The tensions between North and South were made worse because of an argument about the "territories," land in the West that was part of the United States. There was a great deal of this land, and it would be divided into states when enough settlers had moved in. Northerners wanted to prohibit slavery in these territories. Southerners said slaves were property. They claimed that if they moved to the West they had the right to take their property with them to help work their new farms.

Congress had tried to settle the argument by enacting the Missouri Compromise in 1820. At that time, the balance between

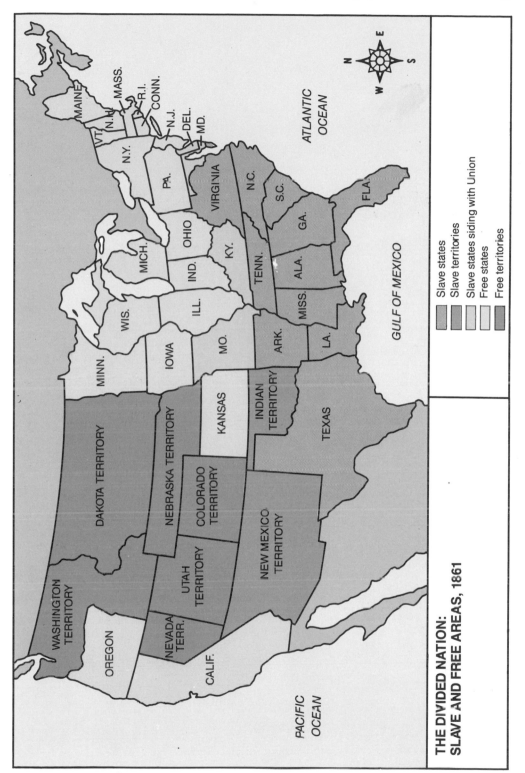

**THE DIVIDED NATION:
SLAVE AND FREE AREAS, 1861**

Slave states
Slave territories
Slave states siding with Union
Free states
Free territories

the interests of the North and the South had been maintained because there were 11 slave states and 11 free states in the Union. In 1819, Maine and Missouri had applied for statehood. Some congressmen had used the occasion to propose laws against the spread of slavery in the territories. Heated arguments between the antislavery and proslavery congressmen had shown how deeply the nation was divided on the slavery issue. Thomas Jefferson had seen these debates as a warning of trouble to come. The disagreement "awakened and filled [him] with terror," he had written, "like a fire ball in the night." Finally, both states had been admitted to the Union, Maine as "free" and Missouri as "slave." However, slavery would not be permitted anywhere else in the territory north of a line drawn west from Missouri's southern boundary at latitude 36° 30'.

The issue of slavery continued to be hotly argued. The huge new territories taken by the United States during the Mexican War brought the argument to the boiling point again. In 1849, California requested admission to the Union as a free state. Again, there were demands in Congress to forbid slavery throughout the new territories. Only by the Compromise of 1850 was the Union once again preserved.

According to the Compromise of 1850, California was admitted as a free state. Yet there were to be no restrictions on slavery in the new territories. A new, harsher national Fugitive Slave Law was passed, which helped Southerners capture their slaves who had fled to "free soil." At the same time, the slave trade, but not slavery itself, was ended in the District of Columbia.

Northern abolitionists, those who wanted to do away with slavery altogether, continued to argue passionately for their point of view. One of the most effective arguments was made in *Uncle Tom's Cabin*, a novel by Harriet Beecher Stowe published in 1852. It vividly portrayed the cruelty and injustice of the slave system. It sold 1.2 million copies in the first year and fed the flames of the argument that led to the Civil War.

Southerners said the story Stowe told was not true, that only a few masters were brutal and inhumane. They said that slaves were

While leaders debated the question of slavery, the slaves themselves worked long hours in the cotton fields.

generally happy, and that they needed the care and protection that white masters gave them because they were not able to take care of themselves. Northerners drew on the book to support their position that slavery was evil. When President Abraham Lincoln later met Mrs. Stowe, he said to her, "So you're the little woman who wrote the book that made this great war!"

In 1854, another step toward war was taken: "The territories of Kansas and Nebraska were organized with the rule of "popular sovereignty." According to the Kansas–Nebraska Act, a new Federal law, settlers could decide for themselves whether their territory would be slave or free. These territories were north of 36°

30'. In other words, the Kansas–Nebraska Act of 1854 meant that the Missouri Compromise of 1820 was no longer in effect. This awakened passions over the issue of slavery once again. One result was that the Republican party was formed to represent those Americans who opposed the extension of slavery into the territories.

Settlers from both the North and the South poured into Kansas and struggled to gain control of the territorial government. Each side held elections, wrote a constitution, and formed a legislature. Each said the other was illegal. In 1856, violent war broke out between the antislavery and proslavery groups, and the territory earned the name "Bleeding Kansas." Proslavery groups put together an army of men who raided the town of Lawrence, Kansas. They said they wanted to "rescue" Lawrence from the abolitionists.

The raid angered the antislavery groups, and at least one man took revenge. John Brown, a determined abolitionist, raided a proslavery settlement at Pottawatomie Creek. With the help of four of his sons, Brown killed five people in cold blood.

Then, in 1859, John Brown brought bloodshed to Virginia. After the massacre at Pottawatomie Creek, he had escaped and moved east. There he planned his boldest move of all to bring an end to slavery. He had a group of 18 men—13 whites and 5 blacks. They would attack the town of Harpers Ferry in western Virginia, where the U.S. government stored weapons and ammunition. Brown's plan was to arm the slaves, who he figured would come to his side immediately, and to establish a black republic in the mountains of Virginia. From there, he thought, he could wage war on the slave states.

At first, John Brown's attack was successful. On the night of October 16, his men overpowered the night watchmen, occupied the arsenal (the building where weapons were stored) and a rifle factory, murdered the mayor of the town, and took some men as prisoners.

The governor of Virginia called out the state militia in Harpers Ferry, and other militiamen came. Robert E. Lee, who was now a colonel, was sent in with a force of United States troops to help. Brown was trapped in a building and under siege for two days.

John Brown's radical abolitionism convinced Southerners that the North was determined to destroy their way of life.

Before the incident was over, Brown saw two of his sons die. He was taken prisoner with four others, the only ones left alive and unwounded after his raid.

The South was enraged. John Brown, they believed, represented the wishes of the North. One Northerner in Virginia, who was wrongly believed to be part of Brown's gang, was lynched, and dozens of other Northerners in the South were arrested or beaten.

The state of Virginia put Brown on trial for murder, criminal conspiracy, and treason against Virginia. The jury found him guilty, and he was sentenced to be hanged.

Northern newspapers called Brown an admirable "martyr" to the cause of abolition. They began to write about trips to Virginia to free the prisoners, and some Northerners contributed money to these plans. Such news made the governor of Virginia afraid there would be more bloodshed. So John Brown was taken to Charles Town, Virginia, where he could be better guarded until the day he was to be hanged—December 2.

Old John Brown did nothing to encourage any plans to rescue him. He told the judge at his trial that if he had to lose his life for the sake of the "millions in this slave country whose rights are disregarded [ignored] by the wicked, cruel, and unjust" laws, then "let it be done."

The terrible national conflict touched Major Thomas Jackson directly for the first time when he was ordered to help maintain order at Brown's hanging. Jackson's cadets from VMI rode into Charles Town with their artillery—two huge guns called howitzers—and impressed all the local militia with their military knowhow. Jackson was proud of his men. He lined up his cadets in front of the scaffold with a howitzer on each side, "an imposing but very solemn scene," he wrote Anna.

Jackson described the hanging:

John Brown was hung to-day at about half-past eleven A.M. He behaved with unflinching firmness.... This sheriff placed the rope around his neck, then threw a white cap over his head.... In this condition he stood for about ten minutes on the trap-door....

The commanding officer announced "All ready," Jackson continued, and

the rope was cut by a single blow, and Brown fell through about five inches.... There was very little motion of his person for several moments, and soon the wind blew his lifeless body to and fro.... I was much impressed with the thought that before me stood a man... who must in a few moments enter eternity. I sent up the petition that he might be saved.... I hope that he was prepared to die, but I am doubtful. He refused to have a minister with him.

John Brown's attack on Harpers Ferry made the Southerners fear for the future. They felt unsafe because they believed the Northerners wanted to attack them and free the slaves. They thought more and more that their only way out of danger would be to leave the Union and make their own nation.

Harpers Ferry, Virginia, was the scene of John Brown's failed uprising.

Meanwhile, in 1860, the Republican party formally stated its position that there should be no slavery in the territories of the United States. Then the party selected Abraham Lincoln, from Illinois, as their candidate for president.

The Southerners supported the Democratic candidate, John C. Breckinridge of Kentucky. Jackson voted for Breckinridge, believing he was the man who could best calm the country. Jackson did not believe the South should secede from the Union. He felt that "it was better for the South to fight for her rights *in the Union than out of it,*" Anna wrote.

As soon as Lincoln won the election, South Carolina called a convention to decide what it should do. On December 20, 1860, South Carolina announced it was no longer a part of the United States. Other Southern states called conventions to consider leaving the Union.

When Virginia called its convention, to be held in the state capital at Richmond, the town of Lexington had a strong Union sentiment. Jackson wrote his nephew:

> I desire to see the state use every influence she possesses in order to procure [get] an honorable adjustment [solution] of our troubles, but if... the free states, instead of permitting us to enjoy the rights guaranteed to us by the Constitution... should endeavor to subjugate us [try to bring us under their control], and thus excite our slaves to servile insurrection [rebellion] in which our families will be murdered without... mercy, it becomes [suits] us to wage such a war as will bring hostilities to a speedy close.

He did not believe Virginia would have to leave the Union because he thought "the Northern people love the Union more than they do their peculiar notions of slavery..."

Jackson worked hard to avoid war. When a national conference for peace in Washington failed, Jackson went to his minister, Dr. White, to propose a national day of prayer.

All efforts to save the Union and prevent war failed, however. Mississippi, Florida, Alabama, Georgia, Louisiana, and Texas followed South Carolina and left the Union. In February 1861, they created the Confederate States of America. (Later, Virginia, Arkansas, Tennessee, and North Carolina would join the others to make up the 11-state Confederacy.)

On April 12, 1861, Southern troops opened fire on the Union stronghold of Fort Sumter, in the harbor at Charleston, South Carolina. Americans were now attacking one another. The Civil War had begun.

Three days after the gunfire at Fort Sumter, President Lincoln issued a call for 75,000 volunteers to join the U.S. Army. This pushed Virginia out of the Union. The state's leaders in Richmond, who had been meeting for weeks to consider whether to leave the Union, declared that Lincoln's action was a signal that the Union would invade the South. Virginia was the first state in the North's path. Virginia would have to defend its land. (Western Virginia, where Jackson grew up, had a stronger Unionist feeling than the older, eastern part of the state where most of the plantations were. The western part broke off to become the state of West Virginia during the Civil War.)

Certainly Thomas Jackson did not fight for slavery. He fought to protect his home state and all the states that felt their rights were being trampled by Washington and the Northern states. A minister who knew Jackson well wrote: "I am very confident that he would never have fought for the sole object of perpetuating slavery. It was for her *constitutional rights* that the South resisted the North, and slavery was only comprehended [included] among those rights."

Jackson was ready when the call to war came. At dawn on Sunday, April 21, the doorbell rang. Jackson was ordered to bring the cadets from VMI to Richmond immediately. He left the house without breakfast to make the arrangements for marching. He sent a message to Dr. White, asking his minister to come offer a prayer for the cadets before they left. Then he went home to eat, to read his Bible, and to pray with his wife. Even at the last moment, he asked God to get rid of the "threatening danger" and grant peace.

Jackson's departure was set for 1:00 P.M. By 12:45, all the guns and ammunition were packed, and the men were ready for the march. They began to call "Let's go, let's go!" But Jackson sat on his camp stool in front of the barracks and waited—orders were orders, and he would follow them precisely. Finally, at exactly 1:00 P.M., he rose and issued his first order: "Right face! By file, left march!"

THE CALL TO ARMS

"There is Jackson standing like a stone wall..."
CONFEDERATE GENERAL BARNARD BEE

resident Lincoln hoped that the war would be brief. He originally called for 90-day volunteers to join the Union army, hoping that the rebellion would be crushed in that time. It quickly became clear, however, that the war would last longer. Both sides knew what they wanted. The South wanted independence, and Southern men had already proved they were willing to fight and die for their homelands. The North was fighting to preserve the Union. This meant invading the South and fighting a series of difficult, exhausting battles.

Because they had different objectives, the two sides used very different strategies. The Confederate president, Jefferson Davis, decided to fight a defensive war. The Southern generals knew it took fewer men to defend a position than to attack. Also, with most of the war fought in the South, they would have the advantage of knowing the terrain.

The North, on the other hand, was committed to taking the offensive. General Winfield Scott, Lincoln's first commander, devised a strategy called the Anaconda Plan. The anaconda is a snake that crushes its victims by coiling around them. The plan was to surround the South with land and sea forces, thereby "strangling" it. It was a good plan, but in 1861 President Lincoln did not realize it would take four long years to work.

Major Thomas J. Jackson and his cadets were first assigned to drill volunteers in Richmond, but soon Jackson was promoted to colonel and reassigned to Harpers Ferry.

When Virginia seceded from the Union, Harpers Ferry was defended by only 50 Federal troops. Confederate volunteers and militia immediately set off to take possession of the town for Virginia. Harpers Ferry had the Federal arsenal and manufactured guns for the United States. Also, its location made it important to the war effort of Virginia and thus the Confederacy. It lay right on the border with Maryland, which was a "border state" that had a population strongly divided between secessionists and unionists, although eventually it decided to stay within the Union. Harpers Ferry was also just a few miles north of Washington, D.C., where the Potomac and Shenandoah rivers meet. With its bridges, railroad tracks, and roads, it was vitally important to the war effort.

When Jackson arrived in Harpers Ferry, he had two tasks: to ship all the arms-making machinery south for use by the Confederacy, and to train the raw militia and volunteers into a real army, able to fight and defend the South.

Colonel Jackson did not look like a commander. He wore a wrinkled uniform that had no gold trim or decorations, his old cadet cap was pulled down over his eyes, and, with his big, awkward feet and hands, he looked uncomfortable on horseback. He never smiled, and he had a wooden or sleepy look on his face. He seemed uncomfortable when he talked. Also, he sucked lemons all the time. He felt it was good for his health.

Jackson made no speeches. He did not inspect his troops, and he gave very brief orders. He never had casual conversations with his men, so that even his officers were in the dark about what he was planning. He believed that if he told anyone, there was always a risk that the enemy would somehow find out what he had in mind. Altogether, one officer said, "There must be some mistake about him."

But Jackson knew what he was about. In three weeks he made an army. He pulled together the 8,000 men, and when Richmond could not send supplies for them, he found them food and clothing and equipment. Jackson drilled his men, put them through target practice, assigned them to guard duty, and drilled them again. He would wake them up at 5:00 A.M. and have them working for 17 hours a day.

He had all the arms-making machinery loaded on trains and wagons and sent to Richmond. He ordered 1,000 muskets, to be manufactured in Lexington. He tried to buy horses for the army's wagons on credit—that is, to buy now but pay later. When horse traders refused to sell on credit, Jackson "impressed" the horses—that is, he simply took them for service with the army.

One day Jackson noticed a small, gentle, light brown horse. Thinking the horse would be a nice gift for Anna, he bought him. He named him Fancy, but the horse was not fancy. He was well formed, compactly built, round, and fat. He had the same

temperament as Jackson: plodding, strong, never tiring, always dependable. Jackson kept him because his gait was "as easy as the rocking of a cradle," and he renamed him Little Sorrel because of his light brown color. The horse and his rider were not dashing, handsome, or warlike. The soldiers would laugh when their commander loped by. But Little Sorrel and Jackson made a good pair and went through many battles together.

Jackson had to build the defenses of the strategic town of Harpers Ferry, which had heights, or small hills, on three sides. He placed his 16 small cannons on the heights to stop any Federal forces that tried to attack. He had orders from General Lee to destroy all waterways or roadways to Harpers Ferry if the Federals threatened to attack. In particular, he was to destroy the railroad bridge across the Potomac River from Maryland and try to obstruct the Chesapeake and Ohio Canal by drawing off its water.

Jackson had the best scout in the Confederacy to help him keep an eye on the Federals—"Jeb" Stuart. Dashing Lieutenant Colonel James Ewell Brown Stuart of the cavalry came to Harpers Ferry from Indian duty on the western plains. With 300 fellow troopers, he would ride hard around the back roads near Harpers Ferry, impressing the Federals because he was quick and quiet. When he returned to camp, he would sweep off his big hat with the black ostrich plume, remove his dusty cloak, and reveal a beautiful Confederate gray uniform lined with red silk. He had a French saber stuck in his golden sash, and he wore a red rose in his coat and white buckskin gloves.

Jackson admired him. Not only was Jeb Stuart vitally important for information about the enemy's movements, but he also understood orders and would carry them out faithfully. At the same time, he could think for himself. Also, he was a teetotaler—like Jackson, he drank no alcohol. And he was as serious about observing the Sabbath as Jackson was.

Jackson organized and supplied the army, built up the town's defenses, and gathered intelligence—information—about the enemy. But he also did something else that was very important.

In those days, railroad tracks were built with different gauges— that is, the distance between rails could vary a great deal from one railroad to another. The Confederacy did not have many engines and cars to use on their railroads. But if they could get trains that would fit their tracks, their war effort would be greatly helped. For one thing, they could send and receive supplies much more easily and quickly.

The Baltimore and Ohio (B & O) Railroad crossed the Potomac River at Harpers Ferry. The railroad was used to transport coal from Pennsylvania to Maryland. It was also kept very busy supplying goods that benefited the North. Rather than blow up the tracks, Jackson decided to "kidnap" about 400 B & O engines and cars that fit the Southern railroad tracks. Since those were about all the engines and cars owned by the B & O, it temporarily shut down the railroad.

Jackson's fame was growing. A Richmond newspaper reported:

> The commanding officer at Harpers Ferry is worthy of the name he bears, for 'Old Hickory' [Andrew Jackson] himself was not a more determined, iron-nerved man than he.... His whole life has been a preparation for this struggle.
> A brother officer says of him, 'He does not know fear!' Above all, he is a devoted Christian, and the strongest man becomes stronger when his heart is pure and his hands are clean.

Soon after Richmond became the capital city of the Confederacy, the government sent Brigadier General Joseph E. Johnston to Harpers Ferry to take command. Jackson was placed in charge of one of the three brigades that patrolled Harpers Ferry and were to delay any advances attempted by the Federals. (A brigade is a large unit within an army and has its own headquarters, infantry, and artillery.) Jackson's First Brigade took over Bolivar Heights, Virginia.

On July 2, Jeb Stuart sent word to Jackson that the Union army was crossing the Potomac. "Old Jack" promptly moved his men forward to feel out the enemy. Then the men fell back under cover of the cavalry. At a church at Falling Waters, Virginia, Jackson's men fired suddenly at the unprepared Federals and then charged

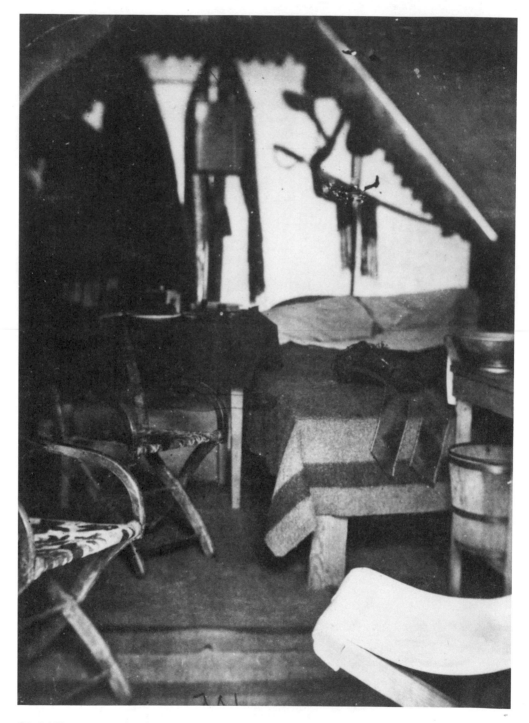

Civil War generals directed battle from their field tents.

them. But the Federals brought in reinforcements, so the Confederates had to fall back.

When the big Confederate guns arrived, legend has it that Jackson raised his head and prayed, "Lord have mercy on their souls." Then the guns tore into the Union line. Jackson wrote: "My cannon fired only eight times, while the enemy fired about thirty-five times," but the Confederates first fire "was probably worth more than all of theirs."

Jackson lost only 25 men—"My officers and men behaved beautifully, and were anxious for a battle, this being only a skirmish [a small fight]"—and Jeb Stuart took 50 prisoners. They closed the roads on all sides of the Federals, and confused the Union commander so much that he thought he had faced 3,500 Rebels, as the Union often called the Confederates. Yet Jackson had actually commanded fewer than 500 men.

Shortly afterward, Jackson received word of his promotion to brigadier general in the Confederate army.

To Jackson's great disappointment, his victory at Falling Waters did no good. General Johnston decided to abandon Harpers Ferry because the Federal army was much larger, and the lack of ammunition made him fearful.

Soon the main Federal army entered Virginia, moving to meet the forces of the South's General Pierre Gustave Toutant Beauregard. General Beauregard, the hero of Fort Sumter, was moving his army northward from South Carolina. For now his troops had settled at the town of Manassas Junction, 30 miles from Washington. This was more than just a threat to Washington. The town was an important railroad junction, it was on the Federal way to Richmond, and it was a point that linked the Confederate armies in the West with those of the East.

General Johnston received a telegram from Richmond on July 18: "General Beauregard is attacked." Johnston's Army of the Shenandoah was needed. Johnston's army had to get away from the heavier Federal forces in order to move east. It also had to try to delay the Federal army from reaching Manassas.

Leaving Jeb Stuart's cavalry as a screen, the army began a quick and secret departure out of their camps. They marched 18 hours to the Blue Ridge Mountains. Jackson's First Brigade led the way. At 2:00 A.M. on July 19, they had crossed the Blue Ridge. The exhausted men simply collapsed on the ground, too sleepy even to think of food.

They reached Manassas Junction the next afternoon and were soon in position on the field behind Beauregard's army, ready for the Federals.

They heard cannon firing, but the Southern army saw few of the enemy. They knew the Federals were there in force: General Irvin McDowell was said to have 35,000 men. They were camped across a creek known as Bull Run. (The North used the names of the bodies of water, the South the names of towns or other land identification to name the scenes of battles.) Hence, the South called Bull Run Manassas, after a nearby town.

On the Federals' side, an endless stream of carriages from Washington carrying congressmen with their wives and other sightseers had overrun the field to watch the action.

Beauregard had 25,000 men stretched along the small river waiting for an attack. He did not like the defensive position, so he created a plan to assault the Federals around their left side. While General Lee anxiously waited in Richmond, President Jefferson Davis hung around the field headquarters at Manassas, looking from Beauregard's face to Johnston's. He wanted them to tell him that all was going well.

On July 21, while he was positioning his men, Beauregard received news that most of McDowell's men had moved far to the left. Then he heard firing, and the largest American armies ever assembled began the bloody first battle of Bull Run, as it was known in the North.

Jackson took a position on Henry House Hill. Jackson's brigade was among 9,900 Confederates defending the hill. He rode furiously up and down the line, seeing that the guns were aimed properly and the fuses cut to the right length. His eyes blazed as he issued his orders: "Reserve your fire till they come within fifty

The intense fighting at Manassas, Virginia, centered around the peaceful creek called Bull Run.

yards, then fire and give them the bayonet; and when you charge, yell like furies!"

When they saw the blue uniforms of the Federals appear over the edge of the hill, Jackson's marksmen, lying flat, were already aiming. When they fired, they blew apart the Yankee lines. Those who survived were driven back down the hill by the artillery and a ferocious blood-curdling shriek that became known as the "Rebel yell."

One of Jackson's officers noticed that his commander was wounded:

The air was full of flying missiles, and as he spoke he jerked down his hand, and I saw that blood was streaming from it. I exclaimed, "General, you are wounded." "Only a scratch, a mere scratch," he replied, and binding it hastily with a handkerchief, he galloped away along his line.

Actually, the bullet had broken a bone in Jackson's middle finger. To slow the bleeding and ease the pain, he carried his arm raised upward through the rest of the battle. This posture made his men think that he was asking for God's blessing.

Little Sorrel took a bullet in one thigh, but was not badly hurt. Jackson's coat was torn to shreds by a bullet that just missed hitting his hip.

A newspaper reported what happened next:

Bee rode up and down his lines, encouraging his troops by everything that was dear to them to stand up and repel [fight off] the tide which threatened them with destruction.... At last his own brigade dwindled [was reduced] to a mere handful, with every field officer killed or disabled. He rode up to Gen. Jackson and said, 'General, they are beating us back.' The reply was, 'Sir, we'll give them the bayonet [meet them in hand-to-hand combat].'

General Bee immediately rallied the remnant [what was left] of his brigade, and his last words to them were: 'There is Jackson standing like a stone wall. Let us determine to die here, and we will conquer. Follow me.'

As Beauregard counterattacked and the battle turned in favor of the Confederate troops, General Bee received a fatal wound and died there.

When Jackson wrote his wife about the battle, he said, "God made my brigade more instrumental than any other in repulsing [turning back] the main attack." In Civil War history, the First Brigade became known as the Stonewall Brigade. And Jackson is called Stonewall Jackson to this day. Still, he always said the term had been used to describe not him but all his brave and victorious men.

General Beauregard commended Jackson as "an able, fearless soldier." In October 1861, Jackson would be promoted to major general.

McDowell's army had been thoroughly beaten and ran in retreat. Jackson was very annoyed that he was not allowed to pursue it. While he was having his finger treated at the field hospital later on

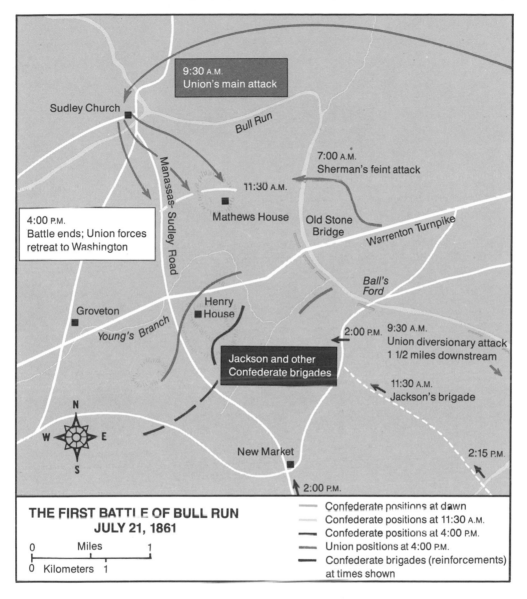

9:30 A.M.
Union's main attack

Sudley Church

Bull Run

7:00 A.M.
Sherman's feint attack

11:30 A.M.

Manassas-Sudley Road

Mathews House

Old Stone Bridge

Warrenton Turnpike

4:00 P.M.
Battle ends; Union forces retreat to Washington

Ball's Ford

Groveton

Young's Branch

Henry House

Jackson and other Confederate brigades

2:00 P.M.

9:30 A.M.
Union diversionary attack
1 1/2 miles downstream

11:30 A.M.
Jackson's brigade

N
W   E
S

New Market

2:15 P.M.

2:00 P.M.

2:00 P.M.

THE FIRST BATTLE OF BULL RUN
JULY 21, 1861

0   Miles   1
0   Kilometers   1

—— Confederate positions at dawn
—— Confederate positions at 11:30 A.M.
—— Confederate positions at 4:00 P.M.
—— Union positions at 4:00 P.M.
—— Confederate brigades (reinforcements) at times shown

the day of the battle, he is said to have told the surgeon, "If they will let me, I'll march my Brigade into Washington tonight."

There were many explanations for why the Confederates did not go after the Yankees, as they called the Union side. The Rebels' army needed reorganizing, there were not enough supplies or transportation, and they would have to cross the mile-wide Potomac River, which had only one bridge and was patrolled by gunboats. Also, the Confederates wanted to limit the war to a defense of Southern land.

Yet it would have been wiser to destroy the retreating army than to let it regroup and then have to attack it again. The mistake would be expensive for the South.

EAGERNESS IN THE TRENCHES

"We are marching to the field, boys, we're going
    to the fight,
Shouting the battle-cry of freedom."

"The Battle Cry of Freedom,"
A SONG BY GEORGE F. ROOT

Spirits were high in the early days of the Civil War. The common soldiers were men and boys who had left their farms and families to fight for their country. Most Americans of that time were loyal to their state first and the nation second. The phrase "my country" was often used to mean "my state." It was not surprising that men were eager to sign up to join a war in which Americans would fight each other, for regional loyalties were strong.

From the moment each Southern state left the Union, there were celebrations in the streets of its cities. Mary Ward, a woman from Rome, Georgia, later wrote:

Every soldier, nearly, had a servant with him, and a whole lot of spoons and forks, so as to live comfortably and elegantly in camp, and finally to make a splurge [to show off] in Washington when they should arrive there, which they expected would be very soon indeed. That is really the way they went off; and their sweethearts gave them embroidered slippers and pin-cushions and needle-books, and all sorts of such little et ceteras...."

The Northern soldiers left home equally excited. Women's groups sewed clothing, bands played, and the soldiers marched off singing songs like "The Battle Cry of Freedom":

> We are marching to the field, boys, we're going to the fight,
>   Shouting the battle-cry of freedom;
> And we bear the glorious stars for the Union and the right,
>   Shouting the battle-cry of freedom.

The towns the Union soldiers left behind were also eager for a fight. One Northern newspaper editor cried that he would "fight the Secession leaders till Hell froze over and then fight on the ice."

In the beginning, soldiers on both sides left home carrying heavy loads of clothing and equipment, and they wore a wild assortment of uniforms. Some Federal troops wore gray in the early days of the war, and some Rebels wore blue. This caused some confusion on the battlefield. Eventually the Northern army adopted blue as its official color, and the South adopted gray. Some soldiers headed for war in dashing costumes, featuring colorful scarves and bright shirts. One New York regiment of Scottish descent wore kilts.

Many young men recruited into the army for the first time left home carrying heavy overcoats to wear on the long winter marches. Carlton McCarthy, a private in the Army of Northern Virginia, wrote:

> Overcoats an inexperienced man would think an absolute necessity for men exposed to the rigors of a northern Virginia winter, but they grew scarcer and scarcer; they were found to be a great inconvenience. The men came to the conclusion that the trouble of carrying them on hot days outweighed the comfort of having them when the cold day arrived. Besides they found that life in the open air hardened them to such an extent that changes in the temperature were not felt to any degree.

Most regiments—both Northern and Southern—had not had much training. The soldiers did not see the value of strict military discipline. On marches, some would lag behind, and others would wander off the road. War was a game in the early days, and when the boys got tired of playing, they simply took a break.

The first major battle of the war, at Manassas, woke up the men on both sides like a slap in the face. The battle was a ragged, confused mess of blood and bullets that lasted from sunrise to sunset. Many men on both sides were so scared at the sight of armed soldiers charging toward them that they ran away into the woods. But most stayed and fought. Again and again through the long day, they steadied, aimed, and fired their muskets, then retreated to the back lines to reload. The guns were so crude and inaccurate that some soldiers joked that it took a man's weight in lead bullets to kill him.

The battle ended with the Federal troops flying in retreat and colliding with the crowd of sightseers who had gathered on the hillside. The Rebels had won a victory. And troops on both sides had learned how terrifying war really was.

They also got used to rough living. They stopped carrying their overcoats. Many had brought knapsacks full of clothing and small

In 1861, Union troops such as these were still inexperienced and eager.

items. These too were soon gone, and so were habits like changing clothes. As Private McCarthy said:

> The knapsack vanished early in the struggle. It was an inconvenience to 'change' the underwear too often, and the disposition not to change grew as the knapsack was found to gall the back and shoulders, and weary the man before half the march was accomplished. The better way was to dress out and out, and wear that outfit until the enemy's knapsacks, or the folks at home supplied a change.

Even though the soldiers kept only the clothes on their backs, these were rarely washed. As Private McCarthy pointed out, "There were good reasons for this: cold water would not cleanse them or destroy the vermin [lice, fleas, and other small pests that would attach themselves to the human in unclean conditions], and hot water was not always to be had."

The marches were so grueling that men threw away more than their extra clothing:

> The infantry threw away their heavy cap boxes and cartridge boxes, and carried their caps and cartridges in their pockets. Canteens [small water containers] were very useful at times, but they were as a general thing discarded. They were not much used to carry water, but were found useful when the men were driven to the necessity of foraging [searching for food], for conveying buttermilk, cider, sorghum, etc., to camp. A good strong tin cup was found better than a canteen, as it was easier to fill at a well or spring, and was serviceable as a boiler for making coffee....

Even tents were too much of a luxury to haul along. "Tents were rarely seen," wrote Private McCarthy. "All the poetry about the 'tented field' died. Two men slept together, each having a blanket and an oil-cloth [cloth treated with oil to be waterproof]; one oil-cloth went next to the ground. The two laid on this, covered themselves with two blankets, protected from the rain with the second oil-cloth on top, and slept very comfortably through rain, snow, or hail, as it might be."

Primitive as their living conditions were, the men had more important worries in the early months of the war. One young recruit, S. G. Pryor, described his emotions in a letter to his wife early in 1862. His tearful flood of words paints a frightful picture of the terrors of the war:

"I felt quite small in that fight the other day when the musket balls and cannon balls was flying around me as thick as hail and my best friends falling on both sides dead and mortally wounded Oh Dear it is impossible for me to express my feelings when the fight was over [and] I saw what was done the tears came then free oh that I never could behold such a sight again to think of it among civilized people killing one another like beasts. . . ."

The Valley Campaign, Part I

"The choice of the Government has fallen on you."
CONFEDERATE SECRETARY OF WAR JUDAH BENJAMIN,
TO STONEWALL JACKSON

he battle of Bull Run at Manassas had been a complete disaster for the Union. President Lincoln and his secretary of war, Edwin Stanton, were in a panic. The North had been expecting to defeat the ragtag Rebel forces in head–to–head combat. After all, the North had more and better weapons and supplies, and more trained soldiers. After Bull Run, the Union leaders realized they had another problem on their hands: protecting Washington, D.C.

General Robert E. Lee knew that this would be Lincoln's main worry, and he took advantage of it. He designed a strategy that would force the Union generals to scatter their armed forces in order to protect Washington. The Union generals George Mc-Clellan and Irvin McDowell had a mighty armed force between them. Therefore, Lee knew it was necessary to keep them apart.

At the center of Lee's strategy was the Shenandoah Valley. Union generals McDowell, Nathaniel Banks, and John Frémont had vast armies spread over the valley. If they united, they could take over Richmond. Lee had to select one of his best men to head a small force whose goal was to keep the Union armies confused. The man he would eventually choose was Thomas Jackson.

Meanwhile, life was difficult for the victors of Bull Run. Jackson's men were camped near the battlefield. Reinforcements arrived slowly, and few supplies trickled in. The heat and humidity were oppressive. The water was bad, and in general the camp was unhealthful.

Finally, Jackson sent his quartermaster, the officer responsible for providing food, clothing, and shelter, to find a better site for his men. He moved the army to another encampment not far away. He was also able to find some new tents for his men, and they received their first pay. They could buy fresh chickens, butter, and eggs from the local farmers. Jackson made himself popular by locating supplies of new clothing and arms. The situation improved considerably.

But Jackson was a devil on discipline. He kept the men busy with drilling and artillery practice. He believed that inactivity ruined morale and made men sick. Many of the men requested leave, but Jackson granted no time off except for emergencies.

Jackson worried about his army's relaxed attitude. Victory over the Yankees seemed too easy to them, and Jackson was afraid they would not be ready for tough fighting. He saw the period after Manassas as the most worrisome in the Confederacy's short history.

Therefore, though the men complained, he kept them hard at work. He made the Stonewall Brigade the best-prepared in the Confederate Army of the Potomac.

On October 7, 1861, Jackson was promoted to major general. Meanwhile, the people of the Shenandoah Valley had been calling loudly for someone to take command of their defense. All the attention had been given to Richmond and to protecting the capital city. Their towns and farms to the west were also vulnerable to devastation from invading Federal armies. The people of the valley had in mind the famous hero Stonewall Jackson, who knew them and the valley well.

During the summer of 1861, the Confederate Army of the Potomac had been reorganized. General Joe Johnston had been

Jefferson Davis, president of the Confederacy, used his best generals in the Valley Campaign.

placed in overall command of the department of Northern Virginia, and three districts were formed. General Beauregard commanded one of them, Theophilus H. Holmes the second. Jackson was now placed in charge of the third, the vital Shenandoah Valley, the section of country between the Blue Ridge and the Allegheny mountains.

Confederate secretary of war Judah Benjamin wrote to Jackson, "The choice of the Government has fallen on you—This choice has been dictated…by a just appreciation of your qualities as a Commander…."

Jackson was ordered to travel to the valley to take his new post on November 4. The men of the First Brigade—Stonewall's own brigade—would not be going with him.

One of his officers came to tell him that the men wished him success and "hoped he would not forget that the old brigade he left behind would be ready to march at a moment's notice to his assistance...." The officer wrote, "As I said this a strange brightness came into his eyes and his mouth closed with more than its usual tightness."

Then Jackson said, "I want to take the brigade with me, but cannot. I shall never forget them. In battle I shall always want them. I will not be satisfied until I get them. Good-by."

THE VALLEY CAMPAIGN, PART 2

"If this Valley is lost, Virginia is lost."
THOMAS "STONEWALL" JACKSON

ackson arrived at Winchester, Virginia, his new headquarters, facing a massive job: to create an army. He found he had only a few hundred widely scattered men, some ragged cavalry units, and some guns without men to use them. Yet a Federal army of nearly 6,000 had occupied nearby Romney, Virginia, and was threatening Winchester. On the other side of the Potomac River, even more Federal troops were gathering.

Jackson issued a call to all militia units in the valley that were not yet called up. He begged the Confederate war department for "disciplined troops of not only infantry, but also of artillery and cavalry."

General Johnston gave him more help than that. Johnston prized the First Brigade—the Stonewall Brigade—above all others, and he did not want to part with it. However, when he was promised twice the number of men as replacements, he sent the First Brigade back to its old commander.

Slowly, with constant drilling and strict attention to detail and discipline, Jackson made the militia units of the valley into a real army. And with his First Brigade and General William Loring's troops from the southwest near at hand, he could make plans.

Jackson had always believed that it was better to attack the enemy, rather than to wait for its attack and then fight on the defensive. He had a plan that he was sure would bring victory.

Throughout the winter, the Federal general George McClellan was training and equipping young men just recently brought into the army. He planned to launch an offensive on Richmond in the spring. Jackson wanted to draw the young Union army into a fight before they were fully ready. He believed that if he attacked the Federal headquarters at Romney, McClellan might look at the troops Jackson had and believe that Johnston's army had been weakened. Thus McClellan might be tempted to attack Johnston with green, badly equipped troops.

Also, if he took Romney, Jackson could get the food and other resources of the area for his men. At the same time, the Confederates would have control of the valley. And, if McClellan did attack Johnston's army and Johnston needed help, Jackson could go to their aid, as he did before the battle at Manassas.

Jackson's first step was to attack the Chesapeake and Ohio Canal—an important communications route between Washington and the West. In the freezing weather—it was December 6—he ordered his men to cut the dam and drain the water from a large section of the canal. Federal troops fired on them and drove them away, but they went back and finished the job. They braved the Union bullets and stood waist-deep in the canal's freezing water, chopping away at the wooden supports under the dam. The mission cost Jackson only one man, but the survivors grumbled and wondered at the mental health of the "old man."

On December 31, Jackson's men received mysterious orders— each was to prepare a white badge for his cap, but not to put it on until ordered. The artillery units were directed to load their ammunition and be ready to move at six o'clock the next morning. The men were to take five days' rations—their food allowance— and to keep ready one day's cooked rations. They were also to keep their water canteens full.

They were ready to march. But none of them knew where or why.

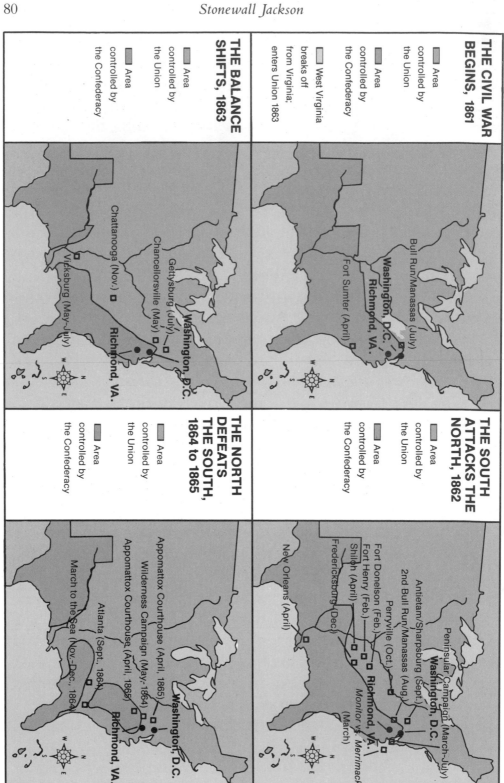

THE CIVIL WAR BEGINS, 1861

West Virginia breaks off from Virginia; enters Union 1863

Area controlled by the Confederacy

Area controlled by the Union

THE BALANCE SHIFTS, 1863

Area controlled by the Union

Area controlled by the Confederacy

Vicksburg (May–July)

Chattanooga (Nov.)

Chancellorsville (May)

Gettysburg (July)

Washington, D.C.

Richmond, VA.

Bull Run/Manassas (July)

Washington, D.C.

Richmond, VA.

Fort Sumter (April)

THE SOUTH ATTACKS THE NORTH, 1862

Area controlled by the Union

Area controlled by the Confederacy

THE NORTH DEFEATS THE SOUTH, 1864 to 1865

Area controlled by the Union

Area controlled by the Confederacy

New Orleans (April)

Appomattox Courthouse (April, 1865)

Wilderness Campaign (May, 1864)

Appomattox Courthouse (April, 1865)

Atlanta (Sept., 1864)

March to the Sea (Nov.–Dec., 1864)

Washington, D.C.

Richmond, VA.

Peninsular Campaign (March–July)

Washington, D.C.

Antietam/Sharpsburg (Sept.)

2nd Bull Run/Manassas (Aug.)

Perryville (Oct.)

Fort Donelson (Feb.)

Fort Henry (Feb.)

Shiloh (April)

Fredericksburg (Dec.)

Richmond, VA.

Monitor vs. *Merrimack* (March)

On January 1, 1862, Jackson's men left their comfortable winter quarters in Winchester and headed northwest. It was New Year's Day, and the weather was springlike. Some of the men simply discarded their heavy winter overcoats; others put theirs in the supply wagons. By nightfall, however, snow and sleet were slashing down at them. Those who had put their coats in the wagons could not get to them when the icy roads caused the wagons to be left behind. The men huddled down, frozen—and hungry. Some of them had already eaten their day's food during the march.

For 15 days, Jackson's army struggled through bone-chilling cold on a 150-mile march in which they went in a circle. The icy roads made it impossible for the artillery and wagons to keep up, and tore the feet of the horses.

Jackson first drove his men northwest, toward Bath, in order to clear out the enemy outpost there. The Federal post in Bath allowed communications between the army in Romney and Union forces in the east. Jackson figured that if the forces in Romney did not know what was happening, they might evacuate. If they did decide to fight, Jackson's troops would outnumber them.

When Jackson's men arrived, the Federals evacuated Bath.

Then Jackson drove his men back down the way they had come, toward Romney. The enemy fled Romney, too, but this time they left behind some valuable stores and equipment.

Jackson then wanted to move north again to cut the railroad bridges across the Potomac River. This would upset Federal communications in the entire area. But the troops were exhausted and almost out of provisions. All but the men of Jackson's brigade were nearly ready to quit. So Jackson left part of the army to occupy Romney, under General Loring, and returned to headquarters at Winchester.

Nevertheless, he had accomplished his major goals. He had taken over Romney, and he had destroyed much of the Union's communication network in the Shenandoah Valley.

Anna had come for a visit, staying with a local minister and his wife. Jackson joined her there, and though he was working out the

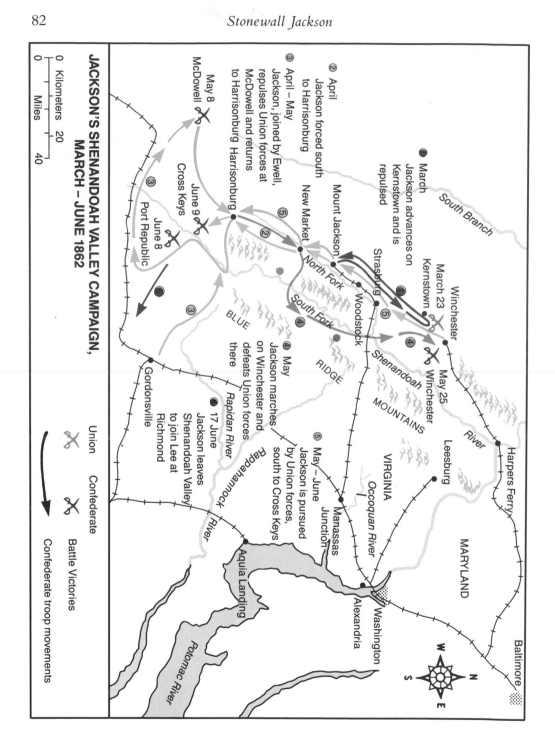

JACKSON'S SHENANDOAH VALLEY CAMPAIGN, MARCH – JUNE 1862

problems of bringing in supplies and other administrative details, he and Anna also enjoyed a brief time of happiness.

Jackson divided up his men and left groups in Romney and at other posts in his command. Driving the enemy out of Romney had given Jackson a psychological advantage, and now he had a good communications network. He could bring his men together quickly if that became necessary. Jackson had grown as a commander—he was willing to take a calculated risk.

However, it could also be argued that a strong, unified army was the only good army, and that his men were too spread out for safety. General Loring's officers panicked. Nine of them drew up a petition to the secretary of war. It stated that they were isolated and in danger of being cut off by Federal forces. Loring forwarded the petition, saying it reflected the "true condition" of the army.

Jackson received a telegram from Richmond: "Our news indicates that a movement is being made to cut off General Loring's command. Order him back to Winchester immediately."

Jackson wrote Governor Letcher of Virginia that he had complied with the order, and that he was, in addition, submitting his resignation. He stated that the order was "in direct conflict with [his] military plans," and that it meant his government lacked confidence in his "capacity to judge...."

Jackson was begged to reconsider. For his part, he brought charges against Loring for neglect of duty and "conduct subversive of good order and discipline." Loring and his "terribly disorganized band" were ordered out of the Shenandoah Valley, and Jackson withdrew his resignation. He had demonstrated that he could not accept what he felt was "interference" in carrying out his responsibilities.

In the meantime, through the winter, the Federals had been moving. They had crossed the Potomac at several points. A concentration of 38,000 troops was preparing to fight Jackson. In the West, Forts Henry and Donelson fell under assaults by Union troops commanded by General Ulysses S. Grant. Southern Kentucky and central Tennessee were in the enemy's hands. In the East, General McClellan was planning an assault on Richmond.

Jackson desperately wanted reinforcements. He wrote, "If this Valley is lost, Virginia is lost." But none could be spared, and finally he was forced to abandon Winchester to the Yankees.

On March 11, Jackson withdrew south to a new camp at Mount Jackson, Virginia. The disciplined conduct Jackson demanded kept his men from giving up. At the new camp, they even regained some of their spirits.

Word came that the Federal division at Strasburg had pulled out and was heading north. That could mean only one thing: General McClellan was reducing the force in the valley so that more men could be sent to join the attack on Richmond. Jackson's duty was to prevent the division from Strasburg from joining the assault.

On March 21, a Friday, Jackson moved north toward Winchester. Altogether he had about 3,000 men with him. He waited for Colonel Turner Ashby's cavalry to get information about the enemy before he made any decisions. He had heard that anywhere from 10,000 to 20,000 Federals were in the area.

Late Saturday night, Ashby rode in to say that Federal strength in Winchester was considerably less than the Confederates had thought, and that the Federal troops there were under orders to move to Harpers Ferry. Jackson's rapid advance meant that he could pin them down.

Jackson was torn, however. He had always respected the Sabbath day, even refusing to read a letter that had traveled on Sunday. To attack on a Sunday seemed like a terrible violation of his faith. Finally he decided. "I felt it my duty to do it, in consideration of the ruinous effects that might result from postponing the battle until the morning."

At Kernstown, Virginia, Jackson put his men in battle formation. He put the Stonewall Brigade, which was now under the command of General Richard Garnett, at the heart of the attack. While Jackson observed the assault from a hill, his soldiers poured heavy artillery fire on the blue-coated Federals, and the Federals fell back. Suddenly the enemy's firing increased, and the Confederates' shots seemed almost to stop—they were running out of bullets. Jackson saw some of his men running toward the rear. Immediately he rode down and stopped a boy who had his back to the enemy. He demanded: "Where are you going?" The soldier answered that he had run out of bullets and did not know where to get more. The general's eyes blazed as he rose in his stirrups and ordered: "Then go back and give them the bayonet!"

The Federal troops turned into charging regiments. Jackson's information from Ashby had been incorrect. He faced more of the enemy than he had expected. To make matters worse, the Federals had quietly brought back another force from the North.

To save his men, General Garnett was forced to order a withdrawal, even though he had not been able to communicate with Jackson before he issued the order. The other commanders followed his example.

Although the battle of Kernstown was not a Confederate victory, Jackson's smaller forces had prevented the Federal army in the valley from joining McClellan for the assault on Richmond.

But Jackson was enraged at Garnett, feeling he had withdrawn unnecessarily. He relieved Garnett of command, had him placed under arrest, and drew up court-martial charges against him. Many in Jackson's army felt Garnett did not deserve this. One private in the Stonewall Brigade remembered, "We had to pay dearly for our reputation, . . . for whenever there was any extra hard duty to be performed, General Jackson always sent his old brigade to that post of duty . . ."

Another Stonewall Brigade soldier, in the middle of a tough valley battle, complained, "I wish these Yankees were in hell."

His friend responded, "I don't, for if they were old Jack would be within half a mile of them, with the Stonewall Brigade in front!"

THE VALLEY CAMPAIGN, PART 3

"Oh, what an opportunity for artillery; oh, that
my guns were here!"

THOMAS "STONEWALL" JACKSON

y the spring of 1862, the Shenandoah Valley was alive with
Federal troops. Jackson believed the only way his small
force could make them ineffective was to convince them
that there were many more Confederates than there really were.
One way to create this impression was to move his troops
frequently and suddenly. He ordered his topographical engineer to
make detailed maps of the whole valley. Using these, he led his
men through a series of quick, secretive movements, playing a
game of "Now you see us, now you don't" all over the valley.

While General Jackson carried out these maneuvers, he also
reorganized his cavalry and tightened up the discipline of his army.
Hereafter, Jackson told his troops, on the long, quick marches there
would be exactly 10 minutes in each hour when the army would
rest. There would be no more stragglers.

In the East, General McClellan was planning a "pincer" movement on Richmond. He would come down the Potomac River
with his troops to a point south of Richmond, and then march up
the peninsula. At the same time, there would be an assault toward
Richmond by troops from the North.

With his clever marches, Jackson used his smaller force to threaten the enemy army from behind. He placed his men so that wherever they were, they could respond to any attack and also get reinforcements if they needed them. Of course, Jackson did not let even his own staff know of his plans, driving his quartermaster to say, "As sure as...I live Jackson is a cracked man..."

On April 30, Jackson sent Colonel Turner Ashby with his cavalry west toward Harrisonburg. He ordered the infantry, artillery, and staff officers east across the Blue Ridge. His own men could not figure out what Jackson was doing. The enemy thought this might be a dash to fight McDowell at Fredericksburg, Virginia, which was on the road to Richmond. Then again, Jackson might be headed west to help fight the Federals there.

Instead, he struck at the advancing army of General John Frémont west of Staunton, Virginia. Although he lost 498 men while the Federals lost 256, the battle was a victory because Frémont's army had been weakened and was in retreat. Now Jackson's job was to keep the army from joining up with other Union forces. He pursued Frémont northward.

The Union commander General Nathaniel Banks was confident of his position. He had placed his army at three points, forming a triangle in central Virginia: Strasburg (which was his headquarters), Winchester, and Front Royal. The spies who informed him about Rebel movements told him that Jackson was many days' march south, at Harrisonburg.

Jackson, meanwhile, saw that a successful attack could be made on the Federal armies while they were split up. With the aid of troops under the command of General Richard Ewell, Jackson planned a major attack on General Banks. He ordered his men northward.

The troops could see that they were marching almost in a circle. One wrote: "I began to think that Jackson was...an ardent lover of nature [and] desired to give strangers an opportunity to admire the beauties of his Valley." General Ewell, awaiting Jackson's arrival, said to a fellow officer, "Did it ever occur to you that General Jackson is crazy?...I tell you, sir, he is as crazy as a March hare...I tell you, he is crazy."

Including Ewell's infantry, Jackson had command of 16,000 men and 48 guns. His movements screened from the enemy, he moved toward Front Royal, his objective. Jackson wanted to seize it swiftly and isolate it so no news would reach Strasburg.

He chose a back road called Gooney Manor to hide his presence from the enemy and to avoid their guns. After a Confederate spy named Belle Boyd informed Jackson that the Yankee force was small and unprepared, he ordered the men forward on the double-quick. Jackson himself was in charge of the advance. The Federals' pickets, or advance guard troops, were driven back into town.

The shocked Federal commander decided to try to make a stand with his 1,000 men and two guns. He took a position on a hill north of town next to the road to Winchester, and placed his guns where they would do the greatest damage. But the Federals could only hope to escape. Jackson raced to the head of his troops, urging them to pursue. He could see the orderly blue column of men retreating on the road to Winchester. He cried: "Oh, what an opportunity for artillery; oh, that my guns were here!" He ordered an officer, "Hurry to the rear. Order up every rifle gun and every Brigade of the Army."

The Yankees took a stand near the little town of Cedarville, Virginia, on May 23. Jackson's cavalry charged right down their center, and the blue infantry broke and ran for cover. They were completely defeated.

Jackson had taken Front Royal. He had captured rich supplies, a Union wagon train, two locomotives, and two guns. Almost the entire Federal force in Front Royal had been killed, wounded, or captured. Now Jackson wanted to knock General Banks out of the fight. Banks, who early on the morning of May 24 had wired Washington, "We shall stand firm," had evacuated his headquarters and was retreating to Winchester.

Jackson pursued. Near Middleton, on May 24, Jackson ordered his guns into action. The scene became like a slaughterhouse. "The road," Jackson reported, "was literally obstructed with the mingled and confused mass of struggling and dying horses and riders." The abandoned wagons with rich stores tempted Jackson, but he drove on.

All through the night, Old Jack forced his men to march on. Many veterans remembered the night of May 24–25 as one of the hardest they ever had. They were staggering from fatigue, and Yankee shellfire told them the enemy was all around. Jackson seemed to need no sleep. One of his officers said it seemed that he was "invulnerable [could not be hurt], and that persons near him shared that quality."

Jackson was driving his men in order to occupy the hills around Winchester before the enemy's big guns could be put in place. Finally, when an officer begged him to stop, saying, "My men are falling by the roadside from fatigue and loss of sleep," he granted two hours' rest. By 4:00 A.M. on Sunday, he had his men up and marching again.

By 6:00 A.M., they could see the blue uniforms of Yankee scouts on the hills around Winchester. Jackson ordered Confederate riflemen up to the hills to attack these men, while he personally led repeated assaults on the Union battle lines. Finally, the beaten Yankees retreated into the streets of the town.

Jackson yelled, "Order forward the whole line, the battle's won! . . . Now let's holler!" And sitting on Little Sorrel he waved his cap in the air and gave a mighty cry of triumph.

Although Banks and a few of his demoralized army retreated north toward Martinsburg, Virginia, Jackson had taken more than 3,000 prisoners, as well as many wagons, more than 9,300 small arms, ammunition, and warehouses full of stores and medical supplies. All this was accomplished in two days, with only 400 Confederate casualties.

Jackson continued his tactical marches, designed to confuse the enemy and weaken it through constant, sudden small battles. He had two more brief but bloody fights, at Cross Keys and at Port Republic, before he led his men toward Richmond.

Jackson's brilliant military campaign in the Shenandoah Valley was one of the Confederacy's greatest strategic achievements. He had kept a Union army of 175,000 from joining in an assault on Richmond. Better still, he had turned the threat of invasion around. Now President Lincoln was more worried about protecting Washington, D.C., than about attacking Richmond.

Jackson was hailed as the liberator of Winchester and the "Champion of the Valley." His fame quickly spread throughout the South and North. In Europe, those who followed the American Civil War—especially military strategists—spoke to each other of the brilliant General Stonewall Jackson.

Jackson himself summed up the rules he had followed in making his most important contribution to the Confederate war effort:

Always... surprise the enemy, if possible; and when you strike and overcome him, never give up the pursuit as long as your men have strength to follow; for an army routed [defeated], if hotly pursued, becomes panic-stricken, and can then be destroyed by half their number.

The other rule is, never fight against heavy odds, if... you can hurl your own force on only a part, and that the weakest part, of your enemy and crush it. Such tactics will win every time, and a small army may thus destroy a large one in detail, and repeated victory will make it invincible."

THE SEVEN DAYS' BATTLES

"Ah, General, I am very glad to see you. I had
hoped to be with you before."

GENERAL ROBERT E. LEE TO JACKSON

George McClellan, the Union commander, was in deep trouble. He had been widely criticized throughout the North for being too slow and cautious. His armies were larger and better equipped than the South's, and Northerners wanted to know why he had not yet crushed the rebellion.

Following Stonewall Jackson's brilliant valley campaign, McClellan's problems were even greater. He had come south with a large invading army, hoping to take the Confederate capital. Now the army was weakened and split into two parts. Still, McClellan thought it was important—for his own survival as well as for the North's cause—to march on Richmond. He still had more than 100,000 men.

Meanwhile, on the Confederate side, Robert E. Lee had been put in official command, replacing General Joe Johnston. Lee saw the danger posed by the presence of Federal troops south of Richmond. However, Lee also knew that McClellan had fewer men than he had hoped, and that thanks to Jackson's skirmishes, they were split into two groups, separated by the Chickahominy River.

Robert E. Lee, seated, was considered by many to be the greatest general on either side of the war.

Lee planned to attack as soon as possible. He called a meeting of his top generals. Stonewall Jackson and one aide rode 52 miles in one night to Lee's headquarters. Soon Generals James Longstreet and A. P. Hill (called Powell Hill) arrived. The door to the conference room closed behind the four generals, the hope of the Confederacy.

Jackson's reputation from the valley campaign gave him the greatest prestige at the conference. Jackson said of Lee, "So great is my confidence in General Lee that I am willing to follow him blindfolded."

Together they worked out General Lee's plan: to strip the city of Richmond of its troops in order to amass 85,000 Confederate men. The plan was to attack the Federals who lay in force to the east and north of Richmond across the Chickahominy River. The Confederates would cut the enemy's railroad transportation and force them out of their trenches to fight or to retreat south.

Jackson and his valley troops would make the longest march, through terrain they knew nothing about, from the northwest. They would engage the enemy, thus clearing the bridges across the Chickahominy so that the Confederate troops could cross without facing enemy fire.

As usual, Jackson had been secretive about his trip to Lee's headquarters. His generals were often confused and insulted that he would tell them nothing about his plans. In response, Jackson liked to quote the German king and military genius Frederick the Great: "If I thought my coat knew my plans, I would take it off and burn it."

Jackson's men began to move on June 25. The terrible rain and mud, and their unfamiliar terrain, made any action very difficult. Jackson spent the humid day working desperately, moving men and wagons along. He rode constantly up and down the marching column of men, urging them on. They were stalled by streams that had become raging torrents and by bridges that had been knocked out. By sundown, the men were still five miles short of their goal.

While Jackson's men trudged through the swampy lowland to join the gathering army, the Confederate forces were being observed from the air. The *Intrepid* and *Constitution*, silk balloons filled with hydrogen gas, were two of a fleet of six built by the Union "aeronaut," Professor Thaddeus Lowe, for the purpose of observing the enemy. Each balloon could carry four men in its basket, which was covered with a network of rope and had a mile-long rope connecting it to earth. One of Lowe's balloons set a record of rising 23,000 feet above the earth.

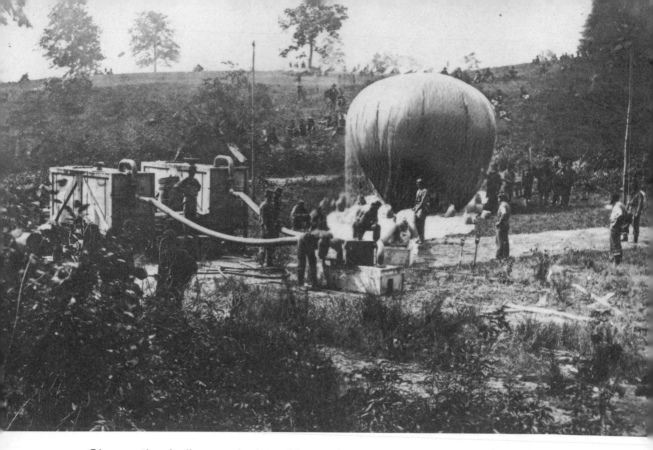

Observation balloons, designed for spying on enemy lines, were one of many innovations of the Civil War.

Although the balloons brought little important information to the North, Lowe's photographs and the descriptions written by George Townsend provided an air view of Richmond and the woods around it just before the battle erupted. He wrote:

> The Chickahominy was visible beyond us, winding like a ribbon of silver through the ridgy landscape. Far and wide stretched the Federal camps... As we climbed higher... Richmond lay only a little way off... with the James stretching white and sinuous from its feet to the horizon... The Confederates were seen running to the cover of the woods... but we knew the location of their camp fires by the smoke...

The Confederate cannon drove that balloon away, but the future value of airships during war was clear.

That very evening, Jackson was delighted to receive a visit from a man he greatly admired, and one who admired him—Jeb Stuart. The cavalry general had just completed his daring "ride around

McClellan." With 1,200 horsemen, in two days he had ridden 110 miles all the way around McClellan's army of more than 100,000. He got exact information as to their location, destroyed or interfered with their line of supplies, and shook the enemy's confidence in their great general. Stuart took 165 prisoners and 260 horses and mules. He lost only one of his own men.

Dashing Jeb Stuart had been assigned to cover Jackson's left flank the next day. He had ridden to Jackson's headquarters to ask if he might assist Jackson in the unfamiliar territory.

Shortly after Stuart left, Jackson was seen on his knees in prayer. Perhaps he then threw himself on his cot, fully dressed, for a few moments' sleep. He had ordered the march for 2:30 A.M.

Jackson had spent two of the last three nights in the saddle. He had had only about 10 hours' sleep in 96 hours, the rest of the time pushing his men toward their position for the grand assault. It is possible that Jackson's fatigue contributed to the way he fought during the upcoming Seven Days' Battles.

The Seven Days' Battles were given the name because for seven days—from June 26 to July 2, 1862—the North and the South fought every day and suffered heavy losses. At the end of these battles, the North had been defeated in its effort to take Richmond and stop the rebellion. But the South had suffered fearful losses from its smaller army.

Early on June 26, Jackson's army was shuffling along the rutted swamp roads, which were smelly and steamy in the heat. By 9:00 A.M., they were six hours behind schedule. Jackson had no good maps, and Stuart was not giving him good information.

In the afternoon, when Jackson heard firing to the south, he did not know what it meant. Generals Powell Hill and D. H. Hill had grown impatient and attacked a Federal stronghold without waiting for Jackson. That was why they were not in *their* positions when Jackson finally arrived at *his* position. Jackson did not know what he was expected to do. Neither he nor Stuart sent a message to Lee's headquarters. Confusing orders had made the situation worse, and the battle of Mechanicsville was the first of the heavy losses to the Confederacy during these seven days.

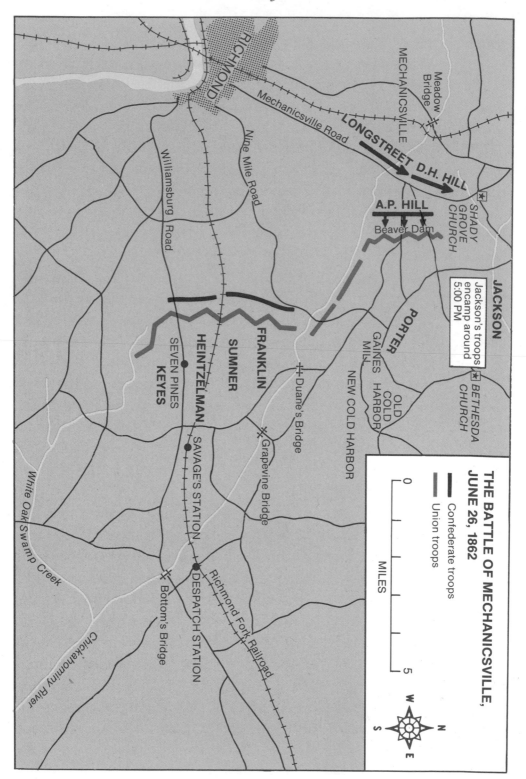

THE BATTLE OF MECHANICSVILLE,
JUNE 26, 1862

Confederate troops
Union troops

0 MILES 5

N W E S

The next day, the Federals learned that Jackson had arrived in the area with reinforcements, and they withdrew. Longstreet and the Hills continued to pursue them, with Jackson in the rear.

At Boatswain's Swamp, the Federals dug in. D. H. Hill was on the fringe of the swamp. Longstreet was trapped in front and from behind and could not attack. He said, "I was, in fact, in the position from which the enemy wished us to attack him." Nothing could be done until Jackson arrived.

But Jackson had been delayed. He had given unclear orders to his guide and discovered he was on the wrong road. He thus had wasted many hours before he reached D. H. Hill's position. Then, to make matters worse, he issued oral orders to be taken to his officers. The orders were badly garbled by the time they reached the officers. They were understood to mean "remain in position and wait for further orders," rather than "advance and join the assault," which was Jackson's intention.

By 5:00 P.M., Jackson was tired and very confused in this unfamiliar country. He pulled a lemon from his knapsack and was sucking it as he plodded down the sun-scorched road. Ahead he saw General Lee. He rode directly to him, seeming to feel no embarrassment that the battle had been raging for two days and he had not yet taken part in it.

But Lee said only, "Ah, General, I am very glad to see you. I had hoped to be with you before." There was not a word of rebuke from Lee for the disastrous performance of his most brilliant general.

According to historian Douglas Freeman, Jackson mumbled a response. Then Lee said: "The fire is very heavy. Do you think your men can stand it?"

Jackson responded firmly, "They can stand almost anything. They can stand that!" Lee then explained the plan of action, and Jackson rode away, sure at last of what he should do, and ready to do it.

In a "voice which rang with the deadly clang of the rifle, he shouted to his staff officers, "Tell them this affair must hang in suspense no longer; sweep the field with the bayonet!" He rode furiously up and down, issuing orders and encouraging his men, then stopping to suck a lemon and frown. The charge succeeded, and the Federals broke in retreat back toward the Chickahominy River.

The reporter Townsend wrote: "An immense throng of panic-stricken people came surging down the slippery bridge. A few carried muskets, but I saw several wantonly throw their pieces into the flood... Fear, anguish, cowardice, despair, disgust were the predominant expressions... A horseman rode past me, with blood streaming from his mouth and hanging in gouts from his saturated beard..."

Many Federals were captured. During the evening, Jackson was out riding with a few of his staff officers. In the dark he suddenly found himself riding into a group of about 15 armed Federals. Figuring they were discouraged and frightened, he spurred his horse forward and shouted for them to lay down their arms. As they marched to the rear, one of them called cheerfully to some bystanders: "Gentlemen, we had the honor of being captured by Stonewall Jackson himself."

There were heavy losses to the outnumbered but victorious Southern army during these two days. But General McClellan, whose excessive caution already was destroying Lincoln's confidence in him, had been convinced by his spies that *he* was outnumbered, two to one.

The next day, June 28, McClellan's troops began a retreat. They tried to destroy all the supplies they could not take with them. But they left behind important war equipment, and Jeb Stuart and the Confederate cavalrymen also found wonderful supplies: eggs packed in salt, lemons for lemonade by the barrel, fine wines and liquors.

They also discovered some Yankee newspapers that said that McClellan was using the wise strategy of "changing his base," and this became a favorite joke. When the men forced a Federal soldier to run away, they would yell, "Look at him changing his base."

Lee had guessed that the Federals were in fact regrouping for another assault on Richmond. He ordered his armies to pursue and to trap the enemy at the 10-mile-long White Oak Swamp.

General George McClellan made a big Union push in the Shenandoah Valley, but it was repulsed by Jackson and Lee.

Meanwhile, Jackson's orders on June 29 were to repair the Grapevine Bridge to the swamp and cross the river to give support in the coming battle. But his men worked slowly, and there was another day's delay.

Jackson was to enter White Oak Swamp from the north on June 30 and join in a major assault on McClellan's men. He was to stop the Federals before their retreat took them to the protection of their gunboats in the James River.

As Jackson's men moved toward the swamp, they took huge numbers of Federals, who surrendered "too willingly," complained one officer, thinking about the expense of feeding them. Jackson responded with a smile: "It is cheaper to feed them than to fight them." Jackson's men alone took 1,000 captives.

When he discovered that a bridge to White Oak Swamp had been destroyed, Jackson decided on an alternative plan. Seeing a good position for his guns on an elevation over the swamp, and remembering the tremendous advantage artillery had provided at Chapultepec in Mexico, Jackson ordered a path cleared and 28 big guns brought up and put in place. The shellfire from these guns was so heavy that one Union general wrote, "It was impossible for the troops to remain...a minute."

The Federal's guns blazed back bravely as their men retreated. Then they regrouped at a new position, one that Jackson could see was much better for them. An assault against them now would be suicide.

Later in the day, Jackson received word that a spot had been found where a new bridge might be built, and Jackson ordered it done. That night he retired, ready to renew the fight in the morning.

The next morning, July 1, the Confederates attacked at Malvern Hill. The hill was near a swamp almost as bad as the White Oak Swamp that had defeated the Confederate plans the day before. Jackson's guns took an important part in the battle of the big guns. The infantry waited, wondering if they would be ordered to charge on the Federal artillery position. By about 3:00 P.M., only a few Confederate guns were still stubbornly firing away at the Union guns on the hill.

The Confederate officers were confused and made serious mistakes. Although the soldiers did their best, the enemy's guns were too well placed, and they seemed to have plenty of ammunition. By nightfall, 5,000 Confederate men lay dead and wounded all across the field and in the woods.

In the morning, Jackson wanted to pursue the enemy. Lee, however, said no. It was raining hard, and Lee did not know where

McClellan's army was. Lee decided to stay near Malvern Hill through two more days.

General McClellan and his men continued to retreat, leaving behind guns and supplies, until they had reached their gunboats on the James River.

Some Confederate commanders wrote in their official reports that they had won the battles and had shaken and demoralized the enemy. Indeed, the campaign that came to be known as the Seven Days' Battles had been a victory for the Confederacy in that the Federals had been driven from Richmond. Further, General Mc-Clellan was disgraced. Before the year was out, President Lincoln would replace him as commander of the Union forces.

But there was some hope for the Federals following the Seven Days' Battles. They had made a successful retreat, and they were regrouping to fight again. In terms of casualties, these battles had been a defeat for the South. The smaller Southern army had lost more than 20,000 men, while the Union had lost fewer than 16,000.

Jackson's were not a large part of the losses. Some commanders whispered it was because Jackson "did not intend that *his* men should do all the fighting." They were suggesting that Jackson had intentionally kept his men from joining more fully in the bloody battles.

Brilliant as the chief commander in the Shenandoah Valley, Stonewall Jackson was not effective when he was only a part of a massive combined battle. On the peninsula during the Seven Days' Battles, the orders he received had seemed unclear to him and he had issued unclear orders to his own generals. The confusion of the huge joint effort against the Federals—confusion shared by the other generals—exhaustion, heat, and the unfamiliar terrain seemed to have interfered with Jackson's ability to think and move quickly, and to bring out the best in his men.

Yet General Lee believed that his brilliant Stonewall Jackson had done everything that he possibly could in the fight to save Richmond.

A Soldier's Life

"Pestiferous vermin swarmed in every camp…"
RANDOLPH SHOTWELL,
ARMY OF NORTHERN VIRGINIA

ollowing the Seven Days' Battles, Confederate troops felt their chances of victory were better than ever. General McClellan was on the run. President Lincoln was uncertain what moves to make next. Robert E. Lee, though facing a mightier foe, was a masterful general. The men in the trenches had good reason to cheer.

But in the weeks following the battles, the Federal government took important steps. Lincoln called for 300,000 more men to enlist in the army for nine months. The Union armies, though beset by sluggish leadership, grew larger and more deadly. The common soldiers settled into a numbing routine of marching, fighting, and sweltering in the heat of summer. And the horrors of war were impossible to forget.

One Union soldier described what it was like to face the attack of Stonewall Jackson's men during the battle at White Oak Swamp:

The enemy's fire was unremitting [constant], and from noon until nearly dark we endured the slow torture of seeing our comrades killed, mangled, and torn around us, while we could not fire a shot, as our business was to lie and wait to repel attacks and protect our batteries [guns]. With every discharge of the enemy's guns, the shells would scream over our heads and bury themselves in the woods beyond, burst over us and deal death in the ranks, or ricochet over the plain, killing whenever they struck a line.... The shot hit some of our men and scattered their vitals and brains upon the ground, and we hugged the earth to escape this horrible fate, but nothing could save a few who fell victims there.

As the months of miserable conditions continued, soldiers on both sides grew tired of their rough lives. One soldier talked of a friend who was slightly wounded and said: "The fact is I would like first rate to get such a wound... Oh! wouldn't it be nice to get 30 days leave and go home and be petted like a baby, and get delicacies to eat..."

There were some breaks from the exhausting routine of battle and marching, however. For weeks on end a company might be in camp awaiting orders. While the generals discussed and debated tactics, the common soldiers rested and enjoyed their free time. Most liked sports. Soldiers of both the North and the South wrestled, boxed, and played baseball. Often the baseball they played was an old version of the game, with only two bases.

But the most popular form of entertainment was singing. Nearly every soldier found music a great relief from pain and struggle. One popular song was "Do They Miss Me in the Trenches?"

Do they miss me in the trenches, do they miss me
When the shells fly so thickly around?

Do they know that I've run down the hillside
To look for my hole in the ground?

Shortly after President Lincoln issued his call for 300,000 more soldiers in July 1862, the new recruits were marching to war singing this song:

WAR TAKES ITS TOLL

When war was announced, thousands of young men on both sides of the Mason-Dixon Line eagerly signed up for service. As they marched into battle, they sang songs like "We Are Coming, Father Abraham" and "The Battle Cry of Freedom." But as the war went on and the scale of bloodshed increased, soldiers longed for an end. Disease swept through the camps, killing more soldiers than enemy bullets did. Especially in the South, provisions ran desperately low. Not only guns and ammunition, but boots, caps, belts, trousers, and medical supplies were in short supply. One Confederate soldier wrote about the marches: "The roads were lined with stragglers limping on swollen and blistered feet, shivering all night...for want of blankets; and utterly devoid of underclothes—if indeed they possessed so much as one shirt!" And yet some of the South's generals managed to keep hope alive in their troops. A visitor to Jackson's army was amazed that his men kept "a fixed and unshakable faith in all he did, and a calm confidence of victory when serving under him."

By 1864, these Confederate soldiers were weary of fighting and desperate for the war to end.

For 600,000 young men, this was how the war ended.

As the war progressed and the death toll mounted, military cemeteries dotted the landscape.

105

We are coming, Father Abraham, three hundred thousand more,
From Mississippi's winding stream and from New England's shore;
We leave our ploughs and workshops, our wives and children dear,
With hearts too full for utterance, with but a silent tear;
We dare not look behind us, but steadfastly before:
We are coming, Father Abraham, three hundred thousand more!

Rebel soldiers made up this refrain after General Jackson's "Stonewall" stand, and sang it to the tune of "Dixie":

There was a Yankee general by the name of Banks
But he couldn't climb over a Stonewall fence.
Lincoln, oh Lincoln how sad was the day
When the Southerns did meet us in battle array
They came in their power their might and their main
And scattered our legions like sheep on the plain.

As the tide of war turned in favor of the Federals, the Confederate troops were forced to put up with greater and greater hardships, and moments for fun became few. Privates were supposed to get $11 a month, which was low pay even at that time. But slowly even this small sum stopped coming. The troops wore through their boots and clothes and got no replacements. Randolph Shotwell, who fought through nearly the whole war, described the miserable conditions of the Army of Northern Virginia:

"It is a well-known fact, and a most disgraceful one, that when General Lee crossed the Potomac [in 1864] *ten thousand* of his men were *barefooted, blanketless,* and *hatless!* The roads were lined with stragglers limping on swollen and blistered feet, shivering all night, (for despite the heat of the day the nights were chilly), for want [the lack] of blankets; and utterly devoid of [without any] underclothes—if indeed they possessed so much as one shirt!..."

Still, it was the summer of 1862, and the Rebels, led by Stonewall Jackson, had won a string of astounding victories in Virginia. There seemed to be hope for the Confederacy yet.

SECOND BULL RUN TO FREDERICKSBURG

"We had the enemy in the hollow of our hands on
 Friday."

PRESIDENT LINCOLN,
AFTER THE SECOND BATTLE OF BULL RUN

By August 1862, Abraham Lincoln had been president less than 18 months, but he already looked much older than when he took office. He had originally hoped to stop the Southern rebellion within 90 days. Now the war seemed to grow more intense with each passing month, and there was no end in sight.

There were two main battlegrounds now. One was in the West, where the two sides were fighting for control of the mighty Mississippi River. Union general Ulysses S. Grant, at the head of the Army of the Tennessee, was proving to be an able commander. And the U.S. Navy had shown some promise as well. In April 1862, flag officer David Farragut had captured the vital Southern port of New Orleans, at the mouth of the Mississippi. Now the Federal strategy in the West was to capture the important port cities farther north. Attention was focused on Vicksburg, Mississippi.

The other major battleground was Virginia, and here Federal forces were in deep trouble. Although the Northern armies outnumbered the Rebels, Robert E. Lee's skillful leadership and Stonewall Jackson's brilliant maneuvering had confused and divided the Federals.

Stonewall Jackson was one of the most brilliant strategists of the Civil War.

Lincoln had had enough of General McClellan's cautious leadership. He kept McClellan in command of the Army of the Potomac, but brought Major General Henry Halleck from the West to lead the overall effort in Virginia. Halleck had won important victories in the West, but there was a difference between him and men such as Jackson, Lee, and Jeb Stuart. The three great Southern generals had an unerring battlefield sense and a gutsy determination to win. Halleck was more of a scholar. In fact, his nickname was "Old Brains." He preferred to fight wars according to textbooks, and he had even written books on military tactics.

Halleck saw that the Federal armies were scattered across Virginia. His first order was to recall McClellan's troops to Washington in order to reorganize. On paper this seemed like a good plan, but it meant that one Federal army, led by General Pope, would be alone in the field for several weeks. General Lee saw this and at once ordered Jackson to attack Pope.

After the Seven Days' Battles, Stonewall Jackson was ordered to take his army to Gordonsville, northwest of Richmond, to protect the capital from Pope's army. On August 6, Jackson received word that Pope had divided his army. Jackson moved toward Pope's weakened army at Culpeper, and on August 9, they clashed with Pope's advance guard at Cedar Mountain and dealt them heavy losses. Pope's main army moved in, but by then Jackson had joined up with Lee. Now two vast armies faced one another across the Rappahannock River, each waiting for the moment to strike.

At this point, General Lee did something that bookish General Halleck would never have done. Military textbooks all said that in the presence of the enemy, a general should never divide his forces. But Lee used Pope's unsuccessful tactic to defeat him again. He therefore sent Jackson, at the head of 25,000 men, on a daring march around the Bull Run Mountains.

Two days later, on August 26, Jackson's men appeared as if out of nowhere 20 miles *behind* Pope's army. They destroyed Pope's supply base, located at the town of Manassas Junction, then disappeared.

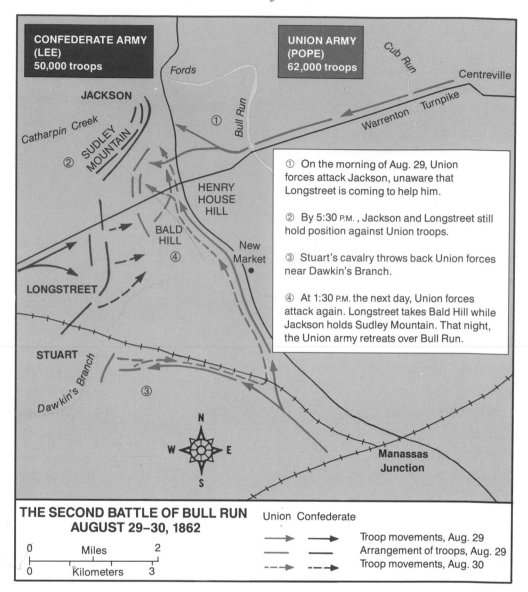

CONFEDERATE ARMY
(LEE)
50,000 troops

UNION ARMY
(POPE)
62,000 troops

JACKSON

Catharpin Creek

SUDLEY MOUNTAIN

Fords

Bull Run

Cub Run

Centreville

Warrenton Turnpike

HENRY HOUSE HILL

BALD HILL

New Market

LONGSTREET

STUART

Dawkin's Branch

① On the morning of Aug. 29, Union forces attack Jackson, unaware that Longstreet is coming to help him.

② By 5:30 P.M., Jackson and Longstreet still hold position against Union troops.

③ Stuart's cavalry throws back Union forces near Dawkin's Branch.

④ At 1:30 P.M. the next day, Union forces attack again. Longstreet takes Bald Hill while Jackson holds Sudley Mountain. That night, the Union army retreats over Bull Run.

Manassas Junction

N W E S

THE SECOND BATTLE OF BULL RUN
AUGUST 29–30, 1862

	Union	Confederate	
0 Miles 2	→	→	Troop movements, Aug. 29
0 Kilometers 3	—	—	Arrangement of troops, Aug. 29
	--→	--→	Troop movements, Aug. 30

Pope was thrown completely off guard. He spun his army around and began to search for Jackson. On August 29, he found him. A desperate fight followed. By morning, Pope thought he had won, and he organized his army to pursue Jackson's men, who he thought would begin a retreat.

But Jackson did not retreat. Instead, Lee's and Longstreet's armies joined with his, having followed the same "back door" path around the mountains. The combined Confederate armies struck at Pope with their full fury. Pope was completely surprised by the attack, and his army was routed. He lost 14,000 of his 80,000 men. Lee's armies lost 9,000 out of 54,000.

The second battle of Bull Run was a major Confederate victory. In Washington, President Lincoln received news of the battle sadly. "We had the enemy in the hollow of our hands on Friday..." he said, and added, "All of our present difficulties and reverses have been brought upon us by these quarrels of the generals."

As the autumn of 1862 approached, Lee decided to capture the Federal stronghold at Harpers Ferry, in western Virginia. From this base he hoped to strike northward into Union territory and begin a major invasion.

Stonewall Jackson led the attack on Harpers Ferry on September 15. The Federals were unprepared, and Jackson captured the base and 12,000 Federal troops. Lee's next move was to surround McClellan's army, which was in Maryland and still making its way north toward Washington. To do this, he had split his own army into four parts. The attack would have been a complete surprise, except for one thing. One of the Confederate officers lost his copy of the battle plans. He had wrapped the paper around three cigars and, by mistake, dropped it on the ground in Frederick, Maryland. It was later found by a Union soldier. When McClellan got the paper, he learned that Lee's army was divided. If McClellan moved swiftly, he could crush the Confederates.

McClellan quickly moved his men from Frederick, Maryland, toward Lee's army. Lee, surprised, retreated to Antietam Creek, near Sharpsburg, Maryland. McClellan had a much stronger army, but he put off his attack for one day while he thought about the situation. In that time, Jackson had gotten his troops to Antietam to help Lee. When McClellan attacked on September 17, 1862, the Confederate army was ready.

The Battle of Antietam on September 17 was the single bloodiest day of the whole Civil War. More than 22,000 men on both sides were killed and wounded on that terrible day. Death came so

Horses and troops face one another across a grim hilltop in this photo of the Battle of Antietam.

swiftly in some regiments that Union general Joe Hooker said, "The slain lay in rows precisely as they had stood in their ranks a few moments before."

Lee pulled back to Virginia. Antietam had crushed his plans for invading the North. The Southern hopes, which had been so high, suddenly fell. England and France decided to delay their diplomatic recognition and support of the Confederate government. (On July 4, 1863, the Union victories at Gettysburg, Pennsylvania, and Vicksburg, Mississippi, in the West, would mean final defeat of the Confederacy's hopes for any foreign help.) And President Lincoln decided to issue his Emancipation Proclamation, freeing all slaves in areas of the country still in rebellion against the United States, to take effect on January 1, 1863.

Still, the Northern generals were unable to deal the final blow. Lincoln had put a new man in charge of the Army of the Potomac,

General Ambrose E. Burnside. Burnside had a new plan for invading Richmond. He would attack Lee at the Rappahannock River near Fredericksburg, Virginia, and then move on to the Confederate capital.

Burnside led his army to the Rappahannock River, but was forced to wait two weeks for pontoon bridges to be put in place. (Pontoons are platforms on floats that are used as temporary bridges.) While he waited, Lee, Jackson, and James Longstreet joined forces on the other side of the river. On December 13, Burnside's men finally crossed and stepped into a hail of bullets. The Battle of Fredericksburg was a major defeat for the Federals, and it offered a small ray of hope for the valiant but exhausted Southerners.

14

CHANCELLORSVILLE

"Cease firing, you are firing into your own men!"

CONFEDERATE LIEUTENANT JOE MORRISON

"All my wounds were from my own men."

THOMAS "STONEWALL" JACKSON

T he thoroughly beaten Federals sneaked out of Fredericksburg during the night of December 15, 1862. Jackson and his army made camp for the winter just south of Fredericksburg. At first, Jackson lived in a tent and refused an invitation to stay nearby at the home of the Corbin family. He said it was "too luxurious for a soldier, who should sleep in a tent." But cold eventually drove him to their comfortable quarters, and here he spent the winter.

Little five-year-old Janie Corbin became his favorite visitor. According to historian Douglas Freeman one day Jackson asked her what had become of the comb that held her hair off her face, and she told him it was broken. He cut the gold-colored band from his own cap, one that Anna had had made for him, and tied her hair back, saying, "Janie, it suits a little girl like you better than it does an old soldier like me."

Perhaps he doted on Janie because of the happy news that Anna had given birth to a beautiful baby girl in November 1862. He had never seen his daughter, but he named her Julia, to honor his

114

mother. He wrote to Anna advising her (perhaps actually he was advising himself), "Do not set your affections upon her, except as a gift from God. If she absorbs too much of our hearts, God may remove her from us."

When Janie Corbin died of scarlet fever in March 1863, the general broke down and cried.

That winter many visitors interrupted Jackson's work, even though he had much to do. He had to prepare his army for the spring campaign, their next military action. And he had to write his formal reports of the battles he had fought. Since the battle of Kernstown, for which he had written his last report, he had been in 14 engagements in eight months. Now he had to take the time to prepare the very detailed reports, and they were not his favorite job.

But some of Jackson's visitors were very welcome, of course. At Christmas, he gave a fancy dinner with the wonderful hams and turkeys and oysters and wines that the adoring Virginians in the countryside had brought him as gifts. His guests were General Lee, looking every inch the dignified and magnificent commanding officer, and his beloved Jeb Stuart, who wore his black-plumed hat and flashy uniform. There was warm fellowship. The others teased Jackson about his luxurious quarters.

Finally, in April 1863, Anna came to visit him with Julia, who was now five months old. They stayed for nine days. Anna wrote: "During the whole of this short visit, when he was with us, he rarely had her out of his arms, walking her, and amusing her in every way that he could think of—sometimes holding her up before a mirror and saying, admiringly, 'Now, Miss Jackson, look at yourself!... Isn't she a *little gem*?'"

On April 29, 1863, the Union's new commander, General Joseph Hooker, crossed the Rappahannock to open the spring campaign against the Confederates. That morning, Jackson rushed to Lee's headquarters to plan for the battle. He sent back word that Anna and Julia must leave the house at once to get the train to Richmond. As they were hurried out of the yard, Anna saw "several wounded soldiers brought in and placed in the out-houses, which the surgeons were arranging as temporary hospitals."

General Lee was convinced that the Federals' main assault would come in the area just west of Fredericksburg. Jackson was ordered to try to meet General Hooker's offensive in the "Wilderness of Spotsylvania," a gloomy area overgrown with black jack oaks, hickories, pine trees, and scrub bushes.

The wilderness had many small trails that led into its crossroads, where the main roads intersected. At one major crossing, in a clearing of about 100 acres, stood a large brick house (often used as a tavern) called Chancellor House. This was Chancellorsville, Virginia, the scene of the upcoming battle.

On May 1, Jackson advanced down the main road cautiously but steadily, his marksmen scouting and probing the woods. Old Jack rode with the men at the front of the troops. Crouched on Little Sorrel as if to hurry the men, he called, "Press forward... Permit no straggling... Press on, press on!"

Jackson's artillery began the fight by firing on the Federals, who fell back and gave no real resistance. Shortly after dark, General Lee rode out to join Jackson at the crossroads. A Yankee sharpshooter sent them running into the woods, where they sat on a log and held a whispered conference. Jackson believed that something had gone wrong with "Fighting Joe" Hooker's plan—either that, or the Federals had not planned a major attack in the "Wilderness of Spotsylvania." If so, they would be gone in the morning. Lee was not so sure of that. In any case, he had to assume that Hooker would be there in the morning and would have to be dealt with.

Jeb Stuart dashed up and joined them. He had learned that the Union army's right flank was weak and could be attacked. Lee and Jackson decided that Jackson, with Stuart's cavalry, would move around to Hooker's rear and attack. Jackson saluted, said "My troops will move at four o'clock," and rode off deeper into the woods to spread out his saddle blanket and get some sleep. One of his lieutenants offered him his overcoat, but Jackson said he would not take it away from him. The young boy then unbuttoned the heavy cape from his coat, and Jackson gratefully accepted that.

Before daylight, Jackson woke up chilled and shaking. He replaced the cape over the young boy and sat down, near a courier's fire, on a cracker box abandoned by the Federals. He could not

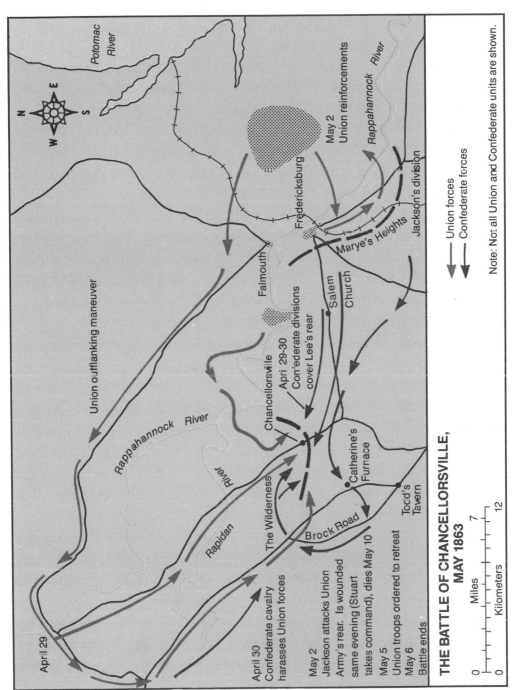

THE BATTLE OF CHANCELLORSVILLE, MAY 1863

Potomac River

Rappahannock River

Union reinforcements
May 2

Jackson's division

Fredericksburg

Falmouth

Marye's Heights

Union outflanking maneuver

Salem Church

Apri 29-30
Confederate divisions
cover Lee's rear

Chancellorsville

Rappahannock River

Catherine's Furnace

The Wilderness

Rapidan River

Tocd's Tavern

Brock Road

April 29

April 30
Confederate cavalry
harasses Union forces

May 2
Jackson attacks Union
Army's rear. Is wounded
same evening (Stuart
takes command), dies May 10

May 5
Union troops ordered to retreat
May 6
Battle ends

Miles
0   7
0   12
Kilometers

Note: Not all Union and Confederate units are shown.

Union forces
Confederate forces

stop shivering; someone brought him some hot coffee. He had caught a bad chill in the night.

Jackson had propped his sword against a tree. Suddenly, for no reason, the sword slipped and fell to the ground. An officer picked it up and brought it to Jackson. The officer wondered if this were an omen of what was to come.

In the morning, Jackson met up with Lee at the crossroads again. It was to be their last meeting. A few words passed between them. Then Jackson pointed straight ahead and rode on.

Moving down the road, Jackson commented to the officers riding with him: "I hear it said that General Hooker has more men than he can handle. I should like to have half as many more as I have today, and I should hurl him in the river!"

In the early afternoon Jackson rode to the top of a ridge, pulled out his field glasses, and saw long lines of Federals lounging at ease, cooking and smoking, and not expecting an attack. "His eyes burned with a brilliant glow," wrote an officer of Jackson's reaction. The enemy had formed itself at Talley's Farm, and next to it was the farm of the Reverend Melzi Chancellor.

Immediately Jackson's decision was made. He issued orders for part of his troops to move into position; he would move in another direction, and together they would attack. He then put a sheet of paper against his saddle and scribbled a note to Lee: "Near 3 P.M., May 2d, 1863 General, The enemy had made a stand at Chancellor's which is about two miles from Chancellorsville. I hope as soon as practicable [possible] to attack. I trust that an ever kind Providence will bless us with great success. Respectfully, T.J. Jackson, Lt. Genl."

At 5:15 P.M., the Rebels crashed through the woods, charging the Union bluecoats with the fierce Rebel yell. Waves of Confederates followed up the first attack. Federal guns could not stop the storming advance.

Jackson rode close to the front on his faithful Little Sorrel. The thrill of battle seemed to have seized him. When he heard a yell of victory, he would lift his head toward the sky to give thanks. When he passed one of his own dead, he reined in and lifted his hand as if to pray and bless the soldier for his bravery. One of Jackson's men recorded: "I have never seen him so well pleased with the progress and results of a fight."

The Federals were broken. They melted away, casting aside their guns and supplies. Prisoners were marched along, picking their way between wounded men who lay under the trees scattered over the farms.

Jackson determined that his final touch of victory over the Federals on this field of battle would come by secret advance. He would put his army between the Federals and the United States Ford, which crossed the Rappahannock River. As he spurred his horse closer to the front, he ordered his lieutenant: "Press them! Cut them off...! Press them!"

Firing by the cavalry seemed to slow down as he rode forward, but he spoke as if the battle were raging and issued detailed orders. By 9:00 P.M., his men were ready for their final assault. He issued his last order—to General James Lane, commander of the 18th North Carolina Brigade—"Push right ahead, Lane," and extended his hand as if he were bodily pushing the Federals back. The attack was on.

Jackson rode through the darkness over unfamiliar ground. There was no light, but he could hear voices. Union officers seemed to be trying to get their troops into line. Jackson hesitated. Was the enemy too strong? Was a night attack too dangerous? No, he decided, the attack would press forward.

Jackson's staff began to get nervous for his safety. In one version of the story, one of his men asked: "General, don't you think this is the wrong place for you?"

His answer was: "The danger is all over—the enemy is routed!— go back and tell A. P. Hill to press right on!"

They were near the North Carolina brigade at the head of the army. Suddenly, a shot was fired. Then a whole series of shots roared through the woods. General Hill's voice called: "Cease firing, cease firing!" Little Sorrel panicked and ran toward the woods.

Lieutenant Joe Morrison, Anna's brother, Jackson's brother-in-law, ran toward the lines and shouted: "Cease firing! You are firing into your own men!"

A voice shouted back: "Who gave that order? It's a lie! Pour it into them boys!"

There was a bright flash in front of Jackson—and he was wounded. His left arm hung at his side, useless. His right hand—

the one he raised to protect his head from the trees when Little Sorrel bolted—was bloody.

He was dazed when his head hit a tree, but he hung on. He couldn't stop the horse. He could barely cling to him. A moment later, a strong hand grabbed the reins. "How do you feel, General? Can you move your fingers?" a voice asked.

Stonewall said weakly, "You had better take me down." He could not help the two men—they had to take his feet out of the stirrups.

They laid him under a tree and sent for a surgeon. Their orders were to tell no one it was the general who was wounded.

General A. P. Hill stood over him and asked: "General, are you much hurt?"

Jackson answered: "Yes, general, I think I am; and all my wounds were from my own men. I believe my arm is broken; it gives me severe pain." Hill took off Jackson's gloves to relieve the pain in both his hands.

A handkerchief was tied around the wound to stop the bleeding in his right hand—Jackson called it "a mere trifle." They tried to make a sling for his left arm.

When the surgeon arrived, the blood in Jackson's wounds was clotted. The surgeon had to decide whether or not to move the general, for moving him might start the bleeding again. To leave him on the front lines was risking his capture—or death by more bullets from both sides that were flying around them.

Joe Morrison rushed away and then returned: "The enemy is within fifty yards and is advancing; let us take the General away!"

Jackson was put on a litter, a stretcher for carrying the sick or injured, and was carried by four men. Bullets hit one bearer in both his arms. Another one caught his handle. Then another bearer suddenly lowered his side of the litter and ran into the woods. Jackson was on the ground with gunshots shrieking over him. Without a word, Lieutenant Morrison and the other men stretched themselves around him to form a wall of protection. Jackson tried to get up, but one officer threw his body over him and said: "Sir you must lie still; it will cost your life if you rise!"

They had to get General Jackson out of there. When they lifted him, he said, "I can walk," and they dragged him into the woods. But then he had to stop; he was too weak. They put him back on the litter.

Back on the road, one of Jackson's commanders, who had also been wounded, came upon Jackson on the litter. He saluted and spoke: "Ah, General, I am sorry to see you have been wounded. The lines here are so much broken that I fear we will have to fall back."

Instantly, Jackson was again the army's commander: He raised his head and said: "You must hold your ground... you must hold your ground, sir!"

The road was dangerous. They headed back into the woods. But one of the bearers tripped on a trailing vine and fell, dropping Jackson on his shattered shoulder. For the first time, he groaned with pain.

They stumbled back on to the road to find an ambulance wagon. It was full, but one of the men insisted on giving his place to Jackson. The other patient in the wagon was Colonel Stapleton Crutchfield, Jackson's chief of artillery, whose leg was shattered.

Jackson's pain had been worse in the broken hand, but now it was unbearable in his wounded arm. He was faint and said he would take some "spirits," but none could be found.

Finally, they reached the Reverend Melzi Chancellor's house. There Jackson met his doctor, who examined him and reported:

> His suffering at this time was intense; his hands were cold, his skin clammy, his face pale, and his lips compressed [shut tight] and bloodless; not a groan escaped him—not a sign of suffering, except the slight corrugation [wrinkling] of his brow, the fixed, rigid face, and the thin lips so tightly compressed that the impression of his teeth could be seen through them.

Jackson told him: "I am badly injured, Doctor; I fear I am dying." Then he added: "I am glad you have come. I think the wound in my shoulder is still bleeding."

The bleeding was stopped and the wound tightly bandaged. Finally, Jackson was given some whiskey and some morphine to control the convulsions and numb the pain from the serious wounds.

It was another four miles over a bumpy road to the field hospital. The doctor kept his finger over the cut artery in Jackson's shoulder, in case the bandage that was twisted around it slipped and the bleeding started again.

The field hospital was at the Old Wilderness Tavern, on the fringe of the Wilderness. The doctors agreed that when Jackson's pulse permitted, his arm must be amputated. It could not be saved, for the hideous gangrene on it meant that it was dying. It might poison Jackson's body if they left it.

Jackson did not want chloroform. He believed, as many did, that if a person was near death, he should have as clear a head as possible when he faced the Almighty. But at last he consented.

In the middle of the night, the arm was severed. It was buried carefully under the earth in a little family cemetery near the battleground.

Meanwhile, the battle at Chancellorsville continued. So many officers had been killed and wounded. But the soldiers fought on bravely. Not the least of the heroes was a 16-year-old infantryman from the North Carolina regiment. The boy's arm hung by some shreds of flesh from his shoulder. He walked up to an officer and said: "Mister, can't you cut this thing off? It keeps knocking against the trees and it's mightily in my way."

The officer cut it off with his pocket knife, and asked the boy some questions about the battle. He answered: "We drove them out of one line of breastworks, and I was on top of the second when I got hit. But oh, how we did make them git!"

Jackson's attack sent the Federal forces reeling. General Hooker retreated with his battered army back across the Rappahannock River.

Jackson was strong, and he was recovering. He awoke on Sunday to receive a message from General Lee: "Could I have directed events, I should have chosen, for the good of the country, to have been disabled in your stead. I congratulate you upon the victory which is due your skill and energy."

Jackson turned his head away and said quietly: "General Lee is very kind, but he should give the praise to God."

On Tuesday, May 4, Jackson was taken, on Lee's orders, to a point of safety within the Southern lines. He chose the welcoming home of the Chandler family, south of Fredericksburg. On the way, the soldiers cheered and called out that they wished they had been wounded instead of their general.

On the journey, Jackson spoke of his memories. Someone mentioned the Stonewall Brigade. Jackson said: "They are a noble body of patriots! When this war is over, the survivors will be proud to say: 'I was a member of the old Stonewall Brigade.'"

Jackson arrived at the Chandlers' feeling strong and wondering how long he would be absent from his command. He received a message from General Lee: "Give [General Jackson] my affectionate regards, and tell him to make haste and get well, and come back to me as soon as he can. He has lost his left arm; but I have lost my right arm."

In the early hours of Thursday morning, Jackson began developing pneumonia. His doctor believed it was caused by the fall from the litter in the forest, which had bruised his lung, drawing blood and congestion to his chest. An inflammation followed.

By the time Anna and his baby daughter Julia arrived later in the day, Jackson was flushed and only half-conscious. Sometimes he gave orders to his generals: "Send in and see if there is higher ground back of Chancellorsville." "Order A. P. Hill to prepare for action...Pass the infantry to the front."

The next day, he was weaker. When one of his doctors told him that he might not conquer the pneumonia, he said: "I am not afraid to die; I am willing to abide by the will of my Heavenly Father." Jackson's calm acceptance of death made it easy to forget that he was only 39 years old.

Saturday was a beautiful day, and Jackson seemed stronger. He smiled happily at his daughter Julia and murmured: "Little comforter...little comforter."

On Sunday morning, General Lee sent a message from headquarters: "Surely, General Jackson must recover; God will not take him from us, now that we need him so much."

But Jackson already had been told he had only a few hours to live. As was the custom, Julia was brought in to him so that he might say farewell. Soon after, he sank into unconsciousness again, murmuring: "It is the Lord's Day...My wish is fulfilled. I have always desired to die on Sunday."

At about 3:00 P.M. on May 10, 1863, just before he died, Thomas "Stonewall" Jackson said clearly: "Let us cross over the river, and rest under the shade of the trees." Anna wondered whether his mind could see the beautiful Shenandoah Valley he loved so much, or was he gazing across the River of Death?

EPILOGUE

A s Lieutenant General Thomas "Stonewall" Jackson lay dying, accidentally shot by his own men, the hopes of the Confederacy were slowly dying as well. Throughout that month, May 1863, a young Union general named Ulysses S. Grant had been winning a dazzling series of victories against Rebel forces in Mississippi. The West fell into Federal hands.

In June, General Robert E. Lee invaded the North in a valiant attempt to force the Federals onto the defensive. In early July, the Federals won the three-day battle of Gettysburg, the decisive battle of the Civil War. Slowly, the North was proving its greater military might.

There had been many brilliant generals on both sides of the war, but by April 1865, there were only two whose actions were important: Robert E. Lee, commander of the Confederate army, and Ulysses S. Grant, commander of the Union army. On April 9, Lee officially surrendered his army to Grant at Appomattox Courthouse, Virginia.

This sketch shows Robert E. Lee after his surrender to Ulysses S. Grant at Appomattox Courthouse, Va.

Lee had given much for his beloved state of Virginia. But another brilliant son of the South had given everything. After Jackson's death, a Richmond newspaper quoted the words of an influential Southerner, who said of Jackson:

"Whether he desired it or not, he could not have escaped being Governor of Virginia, and...sooner or later President of the Confederacy."

TIMETABLE OF EVENTS IN THE LIFE OF
STONEWALL JACKSON

January 21, 1824	Born in Clarksburg, Virginia (now West Virginia)
1846	Graduates from West Point as brevet second lieutenant
1847	Serves in Mexican War
1849	Baptized in Christian faith at Fort Hamilton, New York
1850	Assigned to duty at Fort Meade, Florida
1851	Appointed professor at Virginia Military Institute in Lexington, Virginia
1853	Marries Elinor Junkin
1854	Loses wife and baby in childbirth
1857	Marries Mary Anna Morrison
1859	In charge of hanging John Brown
1861	Joins Confederate army
	Earns name "Stonewall" Jackson at First Battle of Bull Run (Manassas)
1862	Leads Shenandoah Valley Campaign
	Fights Seven Days' Battles
	Fights in Battle of Cedar Mountain (Cedar Run)
	Fights in Second Battle of Bull Run (Manassas)
	Captures Harpers Ferry
	Fights in Battle of Antietam (Sharpsburg)
	Fights in Battle of Fredericksburg
May 10, 1863	Dies of wounds on Chancellorsville battlefield

SELECTED SOURCES

JACKSON

Arnold, Thomas Jackson. *Early Life and Letters of General Thomas J. (Stonewall) Jackson*. Fleming H. Revell Co., 1916. Reprint Richmond, Va.: The Diets Press, 1957.

Cooke, John Esten. *Stonewall Jackson and the Old Stonewall Brigade*. Edited by Richard Barksdale Harwell. Charlottesville: University of Virginia Press, 1954. (Originally written in 1863.)

Henderson, G. F. R. *Stonewall Jackson and the American Civil War*. New York: Grosset & Dunlap, 1949.

Jackson, Mary Anna. *Memoirs of "Stonewall" Jackson*. Dayton, Ohio: Morningside House. Facsimile Reprint No. 32. Reprinted 1985.

Kallman, John D. "Thomas Jonathan 'Stonewall' Jackson." *Historical Times: Illustrated Encyclopedia of the Civil War*. Edited by Patricia L. Faust. New York: Harper & Row, 1986.

Simmons, Henry E., comp. "Thomas Jonathan Jackson (1824–1863)" in *A Concise Encyclopedia of the Civil War*. New York: The Fairfax Press, 1986.

Tanner, Robert G. *Stonewall in the Valley: Thomas J. "Stonewall" Jackson's Shenandoah Valley Campaign Spring 1862*. New York: Doubleday, 1976.

CIVIL WAR

Andrews, J. Cutler. *The South Reports the Civil War*. Pittsburgh: University of Pittsburgh Press, 1985.

Donald, David, ed. *Why the North Won the Civil War*. New York: Collier Books, 1960.

Elson, Henry W. *The Civil War through the Camera, The New Tex History*. New York: McKinlay, Stone & Mackenzie, 1912.

Freeman, Douglas Southall. *Lee's Lieutenants: A Study in Command*. 3 vols. New York: Charles Scribner's Sons, 1942–1944.

Garraty, John A., and Robert A. McCaughey. *The American Nation: A History of the United States to 1877*. Vol. 1. 6th ed. New York: Harper & Row, 1987.

Morison, Samuel Eliot. *The Oxford History of the American People*. New York: Oxford University Press, 1965.

Morris, Richard B., ed. *Encyclopedia of American History* New York: Harper & Brothers, 1953.

Underwood, Robert, and Clarence Clough Buel, eds. *Battles and Leaders of the Civil War*. 4 vols. New York: 1887–1888. New York: Thomas Yoseloff (Vol. 3: 1956).

SUGGESTED READING

Bauer, Jack, ed. *Soldiering: The Civil War Diary of Rice C. Bull.* New York: Berkley Books, 1988.

*Catton, Bruce. *The American Heritage Picture History of the Civil War.* New York: Bonanza Books, 1982.

Commager, Henry Steele. *The Blue and the Gray.* Vol. 1. Indianapolis: The Bobbs-Merrill Company, 1973.

Davis, Burke. *They Called Him Stonewall: A Life of Lt. General T.J. Jackson, C.S.A.* New York: Rinehart, 1954.

*Fritz, Jean. *Stonewall.* New York: Putnam, 1979.

Vandiver, Frank E. *Mighty Stonewall.* New York: McGraw Hill, 1957.

Wiley, Bell Irvin. *The Life of Billy Yank.* Baton Rouge: Louisiana State University Press, 1988.

Wiley, Bell Irvin. *The Life of Johny Reb.* Baton Rouge: Louisiana State University Press, 1987.

*Readers of *Stonewall Jackson: Lee's Greatest Lieutenant* will find these books particularly readable.

INDEX

Barbara J. Bennett is completing her doctorate in American history at Columbia University, where she earned her master's degree and was an associate editor of the John Jay Papers under the late Professor Richard Morris. A graduate of Ohio Wesleyan University, she has taught at Wilkes College in Wilkes-Barre, Pennsylvania, and at the University of Maryland Eastern Shore at Princess Anne. She researched the film "The Battle of Gettysburg" produced by ABC-TV; served on the research staff of Time-Life Books, contributing to the six-volume *History of the United States* and *Life Atlas of the World*; was senior consulting editor for reference and trade books for Thomas Y. Crowell Company; and has contributed to several reference books in the areas of history, political science, and law. She is former managing editor of the *Overseas Press Bulletin*.

PICTURE CREDITS

B&O Railroad Museum: 53. Library of Congress: 29, 35, 51, 65, 71, 76, 92, 94, 104, 105, 108, 112, 116. National Archives: 62, 99. Schomburg Center for Research in Black Culture, New York Public Library, Astor, Lenox, and Tilden Foundations: 49.

Cover: Culver Pictures: portrait, map. The Granger Collection: battle scene.